Kevin Belton's
NEW ORLEANS
CELEBRATIONS

Kevin Belton's
NEW ORLEANS CELEBRATIONS

KEVIN BELTON WITH RHONDA K. FINDLEY

PHOTOGRAPHS BY EUGENIA UHL

GIBBS SMITH
TO ENRICH AND INSPIRE HUMANKIND

To the great city of New Orleans,
which is unlike any other city in the world.
And to the people who have lived here, and to those who
have visited here over the past 300 years—you have added
so much spice to this city, which I love so dearly.

First Edition
23 22 21   5

Text © 2019 Kevin Belton
Photographs © 2019 Eugenia Uhl, except:
page 2, lower middle left © 2019 Monica Pazmino

Published by
Gibbs Smith
P.O. Box 667
Layton, Utah 84041

1.800.835.4993 orders
www.gibbs-smith.com

Designed by Katie Jennings Design
Printed and bound in China

Gibbs Smith books are printed on either recycled, 100% post-consumer waste, FSC-certified
papers or on paper produced from sustainable PEFC-certified forest/controlled wood source.
Learn more at www.pefc.org.

Library of Congress Control Number: 2018960336
ISBN 13: 978-1-4236-5155-0

CONTENTS

ACKNOWLEDGMENTS

WHEN YOU ARE AS BIG AND TALL AS I AM, it takes a large group to lift me up to new heights, but these folks find a way to do it.

Rhonda Findley, you turn my memories into wonderful stories. Eugenie Uhl, you make me want to lick every photograph of the dishes I make. Michelle Branson and the Gibbs Smith family, you take my creations and bring them to life. Austin Faucheaux, Cabral Moses, and Becky Hebert, the work you put in before I turn on a burner to cook is amazing. The Family Crew of WYES-TV in New Orleans, I hope everyone who watches can see just how good you all are through the details, sounds, images, editing, and production. The relatives and friends who help me keep the facts and stories accurate. Deb Goldfarb and Elton Jones, who help me climb the mountain. My city of New Orleans, after 300 years you are still unique because of the people and the culture. Monica, my best friend, my heart and soul, my resource of inspiration, and my wife, you put up with me every day and I appreciate it more than you can imagine. I am blessed.

Thanks to all of you who send kind words and thoughts. I hope I bring a little fun into your day, and a smile.

Kevin Belton

NEW ORLEANS COOKING IS ALL ABOUT THE TRINITY. It's a magical threesome that yields the flavor profile of authentic New Orleans cooking. So it's only fitting that I thank Chef Kevin Belton for the honor of working with him on this third book in the series. It's a window into who Kevin is as a chef, a true native with a deep love and sense of connection to the cuisine and culture of this gem we call New Orleans. He is such a tremendous culinary ambassador for Louisiana. Chef Kevin, New Orleans is lucky to have you as a native son, and I am forever grateful to you.

To New Orleans: for giving me a sense of place and a community of like-minded neighbors who relate so specifically to the food, culture, and history of this beloved city.

To Carlos: for volunteering countless hours to the mission of bringing locally grown produce to our community, and for making the greatest cup of New Orleans' coffee everyday along with other wonderful flavors at our family table. What an inspiration!

And, of course, to all of the strong women in my life: just as Chef Kevin inspires us to turn to our mothers and grandmothers for insight and inspiration, I, too, look to many strong, smart women who make life a joy and learning experience every day. Emma Weber, Twila Pearce Findley, Betty Findley, Sharon Dillard, Deborah Stewart, Karrie Wroten, Fatma Aydin, Ruyevda Collins, Sona Aydin, Elif Taskin, Ayse Aydin, Amanda Zuniga, Terry Gordin, Monica Pazmino, Ashley Schulte, Lynda Barnes, Lisa Suarez, Grace Wilson, and Kristin G. Palmer, thank you for the inspiration.

And to all New Orleanians and Louisiana residents who keep it real everyday by making family recipes and keeping tradition alive. *Merci beaucoup mes amis*. I am proud to call New Orleans home.

RHONDA K. FINDLEY

INTRODUCTION

I CELEBRATE FOOD EVERY DAY. Most people who know me understand that I wake up with food on my mind. Whether I'm planning what to cook on television for my New Orleans and Gulf Coast audience, or the PBS viewers all over the country, or I'm enjoying the simple pleasure of making breakfast for my family, I'm relishing the joy of food. Needless to say, if I'm standing beside my wife in the kitchen chopping ingredients under her direction for her dinner creations, my love of food, cooking, and family is evident. Simply put, food and the making of food is how I celebrate life.

It's important for me to celebrate ingredients and the people who harvest our bounty as well as the events that give all of us a moment to pause and honor what gives us sustenance. It's these ingredients that make up part of Louisiana's culture. Most of the time food, and the celebration of food, rule my life. And I love my life. Being a chef and culinary curator is a life I'm proud to live because I'm sharing it with my family, friends, and the world.

Of course, I need to eat. We all do, yes? And all six feet and nine inches of me can't operate without powering up my palate many times a day. Celebrating food and celebrating with food is the force that drives my life.

It's not unusual for us New Orleanians and Louisianans to include food in all of our events. It's that natural evolution of over 300 years in and around New Orleans that finds our food culture rooted deeply in the bounty of the season, the fisherman's harvest, the weekend angler's catch. These harvests, so strongly ingrained in the fabric of life in Louisiana, mark yearly rites of passage. In Louisiana, it's really how we set our calendars. I've been connected to this calendar since birth.

The culture of festivals and the food we enjoy at these events is an elevated culinary affair. Some of the world's greatest food and music festivals take place in New Orleans. Church fund-raisers have taken note, and the parishioners' annual fêtes follow the rules set by these standard festival bearers: Louisiana food plus Louisiana music equal big crowds. The formula is fool proof. The parish, or county, festivals or fairs celebrate the locally grown or sourced products that vary geographically. The bounty here is diverse, and it gives everyone all over the state a reason to celebrate.

These annual festivals focus on shrimp or oysters or tomatoes or whatever folks identify as synonymous with the cycle of everyday life. And an entire industry of restaurants and food manufacturers sprout around these specific revered ingredients or dishes.

Creole tomatoes become king for two days at The Historic French Market during The Creole Tomato Festival every June. Meat pies are the star of the Natchitoches Meat Pie Festival in September. And there are hundreds of other culinary equals in festival form throughout Louisiana. Most restaurants in the local towns and parishes where these festivals take place include dishes on the menus and manufacture these signature products year-round. Louisiana foodies understand that carrying the culinary cultural torch is a 365 day-a-year mission. And that's what I'm doing in this book—recognizing the great ingredients and dishes of our Louisiana food culture and the festivals that celebrate that food. I've twisted and turned a few things around to create some new takes and true interpretations of the great bounty of Creole, Cajun, and "new" New Orleans festival fare. It's these recipes that bring a taste of local celebrations and put the FEST in your family festivities.

My favorite celebrations are those that allow me to revel in the fact that I'm lucky to be a New Orleanian and can claim Louisiana as my birthplace. Believe me, it's not exclusive to those of us with that pedigree. I'm surrounded by friends who have made Louisiana home by choice. It's no matter. Once you decide it's home then that's all there is. We are a city of immigrants and diversity. The blending and melding of traditions, cultures, countries, and classes are the ingredients we celebrate in our Louisiana cultural identity. And millions of people travel from all over the world for a little taste of that.

With such a plethora in celebrations and festivals, how does anybody take it all in? For me, as a culinarian, it is an intense calendar of festivals every month and every weekend. And these festivals feel inherent and culturally significant. They all have one thing in common. Out of the swamps and marsh and picked from the garden or hauled in from the sweet brackish back bays or briny gulf waters, it's about the people who bring ingredients and traditions that define culture. And that culture is the fabric of Louisiana celebrations and festivals.

Ask me which festival or celebration is the ultimate definition of New Orleans and I will not waver in my response. It's Mardi Gras. Mardi Gras is a city-wide celebration that is not contained to a few blocks or festival grounds. I didn't include it as a chapter in this book because Mardi Gras is so big with so much going on that it would take up most of the book. However, I do want to give you a taste of Mardi Gras, so keep on reading.

When I think of Mardi Gras as a festival my focus is on the family aspect of gathering and celebrating life with your krewe. You see, there are three different Mardi Gras celebrations. There is the adult Mardi Gras in the French Quarter where beads and beverages are on the menu. Then there is what I call the Canal Street Mardi Gras where the older kids and visitors from around the world gather to see the parades roll by. And, by far my favorite, there is Mardi Gras along St. Charles Avenue. It's there in the Uptown New Orleans neighborhood where families gather almost nightly for two weeks before Fat Tuesday. From the newborns all the way up to grandmas and great-grandmas, New Orleans families gather for one of the world's greatest celebrations.

Mardi Gras isn't only about the culmination that is Fat Tuesday. For most locals in New Orleans, and from Houston all the way to Biloxi, it's the season of Mardi Gras which begins on 12th Night or Epiphany. Epiphany is the celebration honoring the three kings who visited Jesus, Mary, and Joseph in Bethlehem. That's the official start of Mardi Gras, and the celebrations last all the way to the end of the festival on Fat Tuesday. The next day begins forty days of atonement leading to Easter. The idea is to party, eat, and drink before you

have to fast and atone. It's a religious festival that has evolved into one of the greatest celebrations in the world.

At the Belton household, Mardi Gras season changed everything, especially the two weeks leading up to Mardi Gras day. I'd come home from school and set straight away on homework. Mom would already have dinner going. We'd eat earlier than normal, and it was exciting to have this different rhythm at home. All of this was done so we could walk a few blocks over to Freret Street, or saunter over to Napoleon Avenue and St. Charles to catch the night parades, stunning floats lit by the men who carried the flambeaux, the lighted torches, illuminating the traditional parade routes.

My grandmother Nan would stay at the Valance Street house to greet family members who came to park their cars in any available spot and meet us at the designated gathering area on St. Charles Avenue. Night after night, year after year, the Belton trinity of three gathered with our neighbors to celebrate in the streets and on the grassy areas dividing the two-way traffic that we call the neutral ground.

We came with full bellies. Mom made fried chicken and potato salad or she would cook a pot of red beans with rice. That was Mardi Gras food for our family. She'd leave chicken warming or beans on the stove in case Aunt Dorothy and Uncle Chet with cousins Lorna and Chet in tow wanted to grab a quick bite before meeting us. It was there for the taking and all were welcome.

Parades were about catching goodies from the float riders. Mardi Gras celebrating was something different, something to look forward to. I loved seeing the other kids, and I looked forward to being with my mom and dad. My fondest food and parade memory is eating peanuts with my dad.

Food along the parade route is still carnival style and is served from brightly decorated trailers with flashing blinking lights. When I was a child, food was hocked from street vendors pushing modified grocery carts rigged with poles and strings teasing you with cotton candy attached by clothes pin from the rigging. Caramel corn, candied apples, and bagged peanuts almost flowed over the sides.

My dad loved peanuts. Peanuts at parades were his thing. Dad always bought us a bag of peanuts to share. And to this day, seeing those bags with the red and white stripes and the blue writing puts a huge smile on my face. It was an experience Dad and I shared. Dad commanded the bag and I'd take a few, run around, catch beads, and come back for more peanuts. It was a ritual that became a tradition born from a festival.

When I took on the role of dad on parade nights, I bought peanuts for Kevin and Jonathan when we hung out on the parade route. I'll buy them for Noah. It's an homage to my dad. It's this simple tradition and memory that marks an event with meaning, a little gesture with big memories. That's Mardi Gras. That's festing.

And now that we are talking about festing, what's a Louisiana food festival without music? New Orleans, after all, is the city that birthed jazz. Food and music just go together.

My mother taught me that cooking is the soundtrack of Louisiana life. I first learned that food and music went together when my family cooked at home. Mom always put on the radio or an "LP" when she stepped into the kitchen. Depending on what she listened to dictated what she was cooking.

When we celebrate the culinary icons of New Orleans, of course you have to have music. New Orleans food is best served with rhythm and soul. There's nothing like red beans and rice with a dash of Louis Armstrong, beignets with powdered sugar sweetened up with a little Irma Thomas, or Mom's redfish courtbouillon seasoned with The Meters or The Dixie Cups.

Together, music and food becomes the social sauce that binds South Louisiana and New Orleans together with the rest of the Gulf Coast and the world. Mom understood this early on. She imprinted this in my soul. But this immersion of rhythm and culture wasn't just at home. We, the children of New Orleans, learn these lessons in school as well. The most memorable cultural immersion as an elementary school student was attending The New Orleans Jazz and Heritage festival with my schoolmates. As a matter of fact, besides Mardi Gras, the first real festival I ever remember going to was Jazzfest when I was in sixth or seventh grade.

I really didn't know what Jazzfest was, but I knew we were going to the fairgrounds to listen to music. We got to bring our own lunch. Remember those flap-and-fold sandwich bags? Mom loaded me up with two sandwiches bagged and wrapped a second time in foil with two bags of Chee Wees (the New Orleans' version of Cheetos), also in that flap-and-fold bag, and two apples. Two sandwiches? I know you might think I needed seconds even as a

kid, but naw, not really. It was my mom looking to make sure everyone was fed. So that second sandwich was in case somebody forgot their lunch. That was the protocol for those field trips. I was prepared even back then to feed everybody. Those sandwiches would be the local Chisesi ham with cheese and topped with a little Creole Mustard. If I didn't give it away, I'd bring it home and Dad would have a snack.

Most children from the New Orleans area, from the early days of The New Orleans Jazz and Heritage Festival, and even now, are lucky enough to attend on a field trip. It was, and remains, the schools' opportunity to immerse children in Louisiana culture.

And speaking of local culture, I really love The French Quarter Festival, and especially what's called "The World's Largest Brunch." Food booths circle the perimeter of Jackson Square with the premier restaurants presenting their signature dishes served in paper boats. I apply the "look, look, eat, and look, eat, eat" principal to taste and try the food. Simply put, you start at one end and look at two booths, make note of what they have, and eat at the third. Once you make it to the end, you go back the way you came, and repeat. You'll get a good sampling of the food that way. I'm pretty much an expert at this, and use this method at every festival.

So my festival eating secret is now out of the bag. It's how I've managed to sample a huge variety of festival foods and signature dishes at events over the years. And boy I have been

fed well! There are more than 400 festivals each year in Louisiana, and that number continues to grow.

It's these foods and dishes that are the inspiration for this book, recipes I've created from celebrating and festing for years here in Louisiana. My hope is that you'll find a dish or two that catches your eye, and that you make and bring it to your next celebration. I hope you find a few different ways to serve food that is simple, fun, and creative. I want to get you talking about food with your friends just like we do here in Louisiana—it's how I've connected with people all my life. It's how I want to connect with you. And I hope you get to experience that feeling. Because it feels really good when you walk by someone at a festival and you look at what they are eating, and something inside of you breaks loose and you ask a stranger, "Where'd you get that?" They are usually in mid-bite and nod enthusiastically with wide-eyed wonderment. And you ask, "Is it good?" This really means,

should I go order that now or later? And more than likely, you just made another new friend. That's really something to celebrate.

It's our culture here in Louisiana to celebrate everything, and in New Orleans we are adamant about preserving our history. We know what we have is special—the architecture, the people, the music, and the food. And we make the time, all year, to celebrate as a community and show that off to the rest of the world. It's these unique celebrations that act as cultural ambassadors to the world. So, let's celebrate together. Pull up a chair and let's *geaux*.

THE FRENCH QUARTER

I WAS ASTOUNDED TO DISCOVER there are over 130 festivals in New Orleans every year. I always thought New Orleans was THE festival capital of the world, and those stats prove it. And I'm proud to say I've pretty much attended most of them over the years. Festing is a lifestyle!

The festival scene is where I learned about the devotion and hard work of restaurant teams. Led by their chef, kitchen teams spend hours perfecting the signature dish, the heart and soul of a perfect festival booth. All of the French Quarter's big-name restaurants participate in at least one of the different French Quarter festival celebrations. You'll find the culinary iconic restaurants alongside the newcomers, dishing up food with the same care and enthusiasm.

If given the opportunity to create a festival food booth in the French Quarter, the three recipes in this chapter are exactly what I would serve. I find great comfort and grounding in the French Quarter and these dishes embrace my approach.

I think Mac and Cheese made the right way—like my mother made it—with fresh cheese, is a New Orleans signature dish. We are all kids at heart, and sometimes you need something comfortable that appeals to your inner child. And Mac and Cheese does that for me, and whole lot of other New Orleanians.

When I take a bite of a fried green tomato, Grandma comes to mind. She made the best ones ever. Putting those fried slices in a paper boat and walking, talking, and dipping the crispy tomato slices in a perfect sauce is the ultimate festival finger food.

Culinary history confirms that Bananas Foster, the ultimate New Orleans dessert, originated in the French Quarter on Royal Street at Brennan's. I forgo the ice cream and turn it into a bread pudding, another of New Orleans' favorite desserts. I love the idea of combining two of our signature New Orleans desserts into one. It's dishing up history, and a history worth celebrating.

Kevin's Take

When you walk through the gates of Jackson Square during the French Quarter Festival, you'll see one of the finest, if not THE finest food booth collections of any festival anywhere. I really recommend that you try to get to New Orleans to experience this event. It's a foodie's top ten paradise.

CHEESY MAC FINGERS

Makes 25 to 30 fingers

---

4 tablespoons butter

¼ cup flour

3 cups evaporated milk

2 tablespoons Creole seasoning

1 teaspoon salt

2 teaspoons dry mustard powder

½ teaspoon white pepper

1 pound macaroni, cooked

½ cup cubed cheddar cheese

½ cup grated Gruyère cheese

½ cup cubed Colby Jack cheese

½ cup grated smoked
    Gouda cheese

½ cup cubed provolone cheese

1 cup grated mozzarella cheese

1 cup grated cheddar cheese

Oil, for frying

3 eggs, beaten

¼ cup milk

2 cups all-purpose flour

2 cups breadcrumbs

Salt, to taste

In a large pot, add butter and melt over medium heat. Sprinkle in flour and stir until combined. Add the evaporated milk and bring to a simmer. Season with Creole seasoning, salt, dry mustard, and pepper. Whisk to incorporate and remove any lumps.

Add the macaroni to the sauce and stir to combine. Fold the cheeses into the pasta until well-incorporated. Pour the mixture into a parchment-lined baking dish and freeze for 2 hours.

Heat oil to 375 degrees.

Cut frozen mac and cheese into 3-inch long sticks. Combine the eggs with the milk to make a wash. Dredge sticks in flour, then egg wash, and then breadcrumbs. Fry for 2–3 minutes until golden brown. Drain on paper towels and sprinkle with salt.

FRIED GREEN TOMATOES
WITH LEMON AIOLI

Serves 4 to 6

---

4 large green tomatoes

2 eggs

1/2 cup milk

1 cup all-purpose flour

2 tablespoons Creole seasoning

1/2 cup cornmeal

1/2 cup seasoned breadcrumbs

1 teaspoon kosher salt, plus more

1/4 teaspoon white pepper

1 quart vegetable oil, for frying

Slice tomatoes 1/2-inch thick. Discard the ends.

Whisk eggs and milk together in a medium bowl. Scoop flour onto a plate and stir in Creole seasoning. Mix cornmeal, breadcrumbs, salt, and pepper on another plate. Dip tomatoes into flour to coat thoroughly. Then dip the tomatoes in the egg mixture and dredge in breadcrumb mixture to completely coat.

In a large skillet, heat oil (1/2-inch of oil in the pan) over a medium heat. Place tomatoes into the frying pan in batches of 4 or 5, depending on the size of your skillet. Do not crowd the tomatoes as they should not touch each other. When the tomatoes are browned, flip and fry them on the other side. Drain on paper towels. Sprinkle with a pinch of salt.

LEMON AIOLI *Makes 1 cup*

1 cup mayonnaise

2 cloves garlic, minced

1 tablespoon grated lemon rind

1 tablespoon fresh lemon juice

1/4 teaspoon salt

1/4 teaspoon white pepper

Stir together all ingredients. Serve as a dipping sauce with the fried tomatoes.

BANANAS FOSTER BREAD PUDDING
WITH RUM SAUCE

Serves 12

---

1 loaf French bread, cut into
  1- to 2-inch pieces and dried

1 cup banana liqueur

2 to 3 cups milk

3 eggs, beaten

1 teaspoon cinnamon

1½ cups sugar

1 tablespoon vanilla

2 bananas, diced

8 tablespoons butter, melted

Brown sugar, to taste

Preheat oven to 350 degrees.

Place the bread pieces in a large bowl. Add banana liqueur and milk, mixing and breaking up the bread so it can absorb both liquids. Add eggs to bread mixture.

Mix cinnamon into sugar and add to the bowl and stir. Add vanilla, bananas, and butter and mix well.

Pour mixture into a buttered baking pan and top with brown sugar. Bake for 75–90 minutes until browned.

RUM SAUCE

8 tablespoons butter

1 cup powdered sugar

3 egg yolks

¼ cup rum

Melt butter in a saucepan. Remove from heat. Add powdered sugar. Place egg yolks on top of sugar and mix well. Stir in rum and serve.

JAZZY FEST FOOD

TALK OF FESTIVAL FOOD and ultimate Louisiana celebrations always turns to the New Orleans Jazz and Heritage Festival, or Jazzfest. Of course, music is first served on the menu, but in true New Orleans fashion, food has become the star of the seven-day festival. Over the last forty years the culinary dishes have become an equal part of the celebration. Food at Jazzfest is like the symphony behind the conductor.

Years ago as a young professional chef, I was welcomed into Pierre "Pete" Hilzim's booth when he created Crawfish Monica™. Crawfish Monica is the favorite dish of fest goers. Pete combined a signature Louisiana ingredient, crawfish, with local culinary techniques to birth a gastronomic phenomenon and trademarked his dish. People from around the world line up to enjoy it.

In 2017, I did my first live television broadcast from the fairgrounds, highlighting Jazzfest and what to see, do, and, of course, eat. The breadth and depth of Louisiana food culture is truly commendable. And it's the food part I believe that is instrumental in delivering the heritage of New Orleans during the festival. The longest served dishes, Crawfish Bread, Crawfish Monica, and Crawfish Enchiladas are some of the most endearing, and the most famous.

My inspiration for Jazzfest food focuses on dishes that define the spirit of the festival, food that people from around the country and around the world can't easily find anywhere else.

My stuffed bread is an expression of that spirit. It has a hidden surprise of flavorful ingredients in warm soft bread that contains the spiced sauce. And the po' boy, birthed by the Martin Brothers to feed those "po' boys" out of work from a streetcar strike also taps into the spirit of New Orleans. Every festival features a New Orleans-style po' boy. I personally love a shrimp rémoulade po' boy. The recipe in this chapter takes a classic shrimp rémoulade salad and piles it on top of crusty French bread. My seafood pasta dish sums up Jazzfest in a classic and iconic way. The recipe speaks for itself.

Kevin's Take
I recommend packing a few to-go containers, and maybe even a grocery bag in your festival gear. Just in case. The idea of picking up a few extra crawfish bread or a serving of Crawfish Monica for later makes the price of the festival ticket more than worth it. It's like an extra festival day in the fridge.

BUFFALO CHICKEN DIP STUFFED BREAD

Serves 4

---

1 (8-ounce) package cream cheese, softened

Buffalo Sauce, to taste

1 tablespoon Creole seasoning

1½ cups shredded chicken

1 cup grated mozzarella cheese

1 cup crumbled blue cheese

3 green onions, sliced

1 pound store-bought frozen bread dough, thawed

4 tablespoons unsalted butter, melted

Chopped parsley, optional

Ranch dressing, for serving

Preheat oven to 375 degrees. Prepare a baking sheet with nonstick cooking spray.

In a large bowl, mix together the cream cheese, Buffalo Sauce, and Creole seasoning. Mix well and then add chicken, mozzarella, blue cheese, and green onions, stirring until smooth and well-combined. Set aside.

Place bread dough on a floured surface, and using your hands or a rolling pin, spread dough into approximately a 9 x 13-inch rectangle. Place chicken ingredients down the center, and overlap with each side of dough. Place on baking sheet. Using a sharp knife, make 4 diagonal cuts along the top of the bread. Bake for 25–30 minutes until golden brown. Let rest for 5 minutes before slicing.

Brush with melted butter and sprinkle with chopped parsley. Serve warm with ranch dressing for dipping.

BUFFALO SAUCE *Makes 2½ cups*

1 cup butter, melted

1 to 2 teaspoons garlic powder

¾ cup hot sauce

¾ cup garlic sauce

Place all ingredients in bowl and combine well.

SHRIMP RÉMOULADE PO' BOY

Serves 4

---

2 pounds shrimp, peeled
  and deveined

6 cloves garlic, peeled

1 tablespoon red pepper flakes

1 tablespoon black peppercorns

1 tablespoon celery seeds

2 sprigs fresh thyme

3 bay leaves

1 gallon water

2 lemons, halved

1 small onion, halved

¼ cup kosher salt

Rémoulade Sauce

1 loaf French bread

1 head iceberg lettuce, shredded

3 tomatoes, sliced

Rinse shrimp in cold water and set aside.

In square of cheesecloth, add garlic, red pepper flakes, peppercorns, celery seeds, thyme, and bay leaves, tying with string and making a sachet.

In a stock pot, add water, herb sachet, lemons, onion, and salt. Bring to a boil, add shrimp, and cook for 3 minutes. Turn off heat and let set for 5 minutes to absorb flavor. Remove sachet, lemons, and onion. Add ice to pot to cool and

stop shrimp from cooking. Strain and place shrimp in refrigerator and chill.

Place shrimp in a bowl and add Rémoulade Sauce, stirring to coat shrimp.

Cut open French bread, add shrimp. Top with lettuce and sliced tomatoes.

Note: I often smoke the shrimp to give them an added flavor. I suggest you follow the manufacturer's directions for cooking time.

RÉMOULADE SAUCE *Makes 2 cups*

⅓ cup olive oil

2 tablespoons red wine vinegar

1 tablespoon Creole seasoning

2 tablespoons paprika

⅛ teaspoon white pepper

1 tablespoon Worcestershire sauce

½ cup Creole mustard

½ cup sliced green onions

½ cup parsley

Combine oil, vinegar, Creole seasoning, paprika, and pepper. Mix thoroughly. Add Worcestershire sauce and Creole mustard

and stir. Fold in green onions and parsley. Chill until ready to use.

LOUISIANA SEAFOOD PASTA

Serves 4 to 6

1 pound pasta such as
  penne, gemelli, or ziti

2 cups heavy whipping cream

2 tablespoons chopped fresh basil

1 tablespoon chopped fresh thyme

1 tablespoon Creole seasoning

³/₄ teaspoon crushed fresh
  red pepper flakes

1 teaspoon salt

1 cup sliced green onions

¹/₂ cup chopped parsley

¹/₂ pound shrimp, peeled
  and deveined

¹/₂ pound crawfish

³/₄ cup grated Swiss cheese

¹/₄ cup grated Parmesan cheese

¹/₂ pound lump crab

Parsley, for garnish

Cook pasta in a large pot of boiling salted water until al dente.

Meanwhile, pour cream into large skillet. Cook over medium heat, stirring constantly, until just boiling. Reduce heat, add basil, thyme, Creole seasoning, red pepper flakes, salt, green onion, and parsley. Simmer until thick.

Stir in shrimp and crawfish and cook for 3 minutes. Stir in cheeses, blending well. Stir in drained pasta and mix well. Fold in crab.

Remove from heat. Garnish with parsley and serve.

QUE UP THE BBQ

I'M A HUGE FAN OF BARBEQUE, mainly because I'm a huge fan of pork. My favorite is pork smoked slowly over a cloudy, hot flame or grilled over real charcoal briquettes. I dream about grilled pork chops and smoky barbequed pork loin.

In Cajun country, the cochon de lait is pretty much Louisiana's version of barbeque. Cochon de lait literally translates as suckling pig, and it's the celebration of slow roasting the meat over a pit fire. In regular terms, it's a pig roast. And a pig roast is a family affair. Friends, neighbors, and relatives gather, and, of course, bring all the accompanying dishes from appetizers to desserts. For some, it's the annual weekend for a family reunion, or a wedding rehearsal dinner. One of the most famous cochon de lait festivals takes place in Mansura, Louisiana, every May. This festival has been happening for over forty years.

A great barbeque festival in New Orleans is the Hogs for the Cause festival that began in 2008 to celebrate the tradition of open flame barbeque. With over 100 teams competing for honors, the event raises money for medical expenses of children fighting pediatric brain cancer and their families.

Two of recipes in this chapter reflect my love for ham and pork, although they are not barbeque recipes. The third recipe has you grilling up some skewers!

Kevin's Take

The Belton's were not a barbeque-outside-on-the-grill type family. Mom had a stovetop griddle that she used. As a single father in my twenties, I bought a grill, charcoal, and a starter. I set that thing up and fanned the flames, and no sooner than I did, down came the rain. I pulled it under the carport and the boys ran inside. It was not looking too good for my first try. But I watched the flames and briquettes go from flame, to glow, then to ash. When I thought it was the right temperature, I plopped hamburgers on the grill and went in and out of the house checking from the boys to the burgers and back. Of course, I let the coals go too long before I put the meat on and we ate burgers that were not stellar. But we laughed about the whole process. And we created a memory.

I'm going to tell you that learning to barbeque on a grill takes time to master. Keep at it and don't give up. There are all kinds of fancy equipment you can buy. I say keep it simple. Charcoal is the key to great flavor.

HAM CROQUETTES
WITH PEACH-PEPPER DIPPING SAUCE

Serves 6 to 8

---

1 tablespoon butter

1/2 cup chopped onion

3 medium green onions, sliced

1 tablespoon minced garlic

1/2 teaspoon garlic powder

1 pound ham, finely chopped

1 1/2 cups grated cheddar cheese

3 cups seasoned
  breadcrumbs, divided

4 eggs, divided

1 tablespoon Creole seasoning

1 teaspoon salt, plus extra

2 cups vegetable oil, for frying

1/8 cup water

Melt butter in a large skillet over medium heat. Stir in onion, green onions, and garlic; cook until tender, about 10 minutes.

Place contents of skillet in a large bowl. Stir in garlic powder, ham, cheese, and 1 1/2 cups breadcrumbs. Beat 3 eggs and stir into ham mixture. Sprinkle with Creole seasoning and salt. Using your hands, make 1 1/2-inch balls out of the ham mixture.

Heat oil in a large skillet over medium heat. Spread remaining breadcrumbs onto a plate. In a large bowl, beat remaining egg; stir in water. Dip balls into egg mixture and then roll in breadcrumbs. Place balls in hot oil, being careful not to crowd. Fry until golden brown. Drain on paper towels. Sprinkle with salt.

PEACH-PEPPER DIPPING SAUCE *Makes 1 cup*

1 cup peach preserves

1/4 cup orange juice

1 teaspoon lemon juice

1 jalapeño, cut open

Place all ingredients in small saucepan, stir to combine, and cook on low-medium heat for 10 minutes. Remove pepper and serve.

PULLED PORK AND SLAW SANDWICHES

Serves 8 to 10

SLAW

2 cups shredded green cabbage

2 cups shredded red cabbage

2 Granny Smith apples, julienned

1 cup shredded carrots

1/2 cup mayonnaise

2 tablespoons apple cider vinegar

1 tablespoon sugar

1 tablespoon Creole mustard

1 teaspoon Creole seasoning

1/2 teaspoon salt

PULLED PORK

1 (4 1/2- to 5-pound) boneless
   or bone-in pork shoulder

3 tablespoons Creole seasoning

2 tablespoons salt

2 tablespoons vegetable oil

1 onion, chopped

4 cloves garlic, minced

2 tablespoons tomato paste

1 tablespoon chili powder

2 teaspoons ground cumin

1 cup ham stock

3 tablespoons apple cider vinegar

1 tablespoon Worcestershire sauce

10 brioche buns

SLAW In a large bowl, combine green and red cabbage, apples, and carrots and mix well.

In a small bowl, add mayonnaise, vinegar, sugar, Creole mustard, Creole seasoning, and salt; stir to combine. Toss with slaw cabbage mixture and refrigerate for 1 hour before serving.

PULLED PORK Rub the pork with Creole seasoning and salt and set in pressure cooker.

Heat oil in a wide skillet over medium heat. Add the onion and garlic and cook for 5 minutes. Stir in the tomato paste, chili powder, and cumin. Cook about 3 minutes. Add the

ham stock, vinegar, and Worcestershire sauce and cook for about 1 minute.

Remove from heat and add to pressure cooker with the pork and cook for 35 minutes following manufacturer's directions. When roast is done, remove from the pressure cooker and place on a platter. Shred roast using 2 forks. If you prefer, you can reserve 1/2 cup of the drippings from the cooker and combine the shredded meat.

Place slaw on the bottom of the buns and top with pulled pork. Extra sauce can be used on the top buns before placing on the pork.

ASIAN BEEF SKEWERS

Serves 4

1½ pounds top sirloin steak

1 tablespoon Creole seasoning

1 red onion

²/₃ cup soy sauce

6 cloves garlic, minced

¼ cup sesame oil

½ cup vegetable oil

½ cup sugar

1 tablespoon grated ginger

2 tablespoons sesame seeds

Skewers, soaked in water

Sliced green onions, for garnish

Cut steak into 1-inch cubes and season with Creole seasoning. Cut the red onion into large chunks and set aside.

In a large bowl, whisk together soy sauce, garlic, sesame oil, vegetable oil, sugar, ginger, and sesame seeds. Add the steak and toss to coat. Marinate for at least 3 hours or overnight in the refrigerator.

Preheat a grill or skillet to medium-high heat. Thread the meat and the red onion onto the skewers. Grill for 8–10 minutes until the meat is done to liking. Sprinkle with green onions and serve.

THE OYSTER FEST

AROUND 1985 WITH MY TOUR GUIDE CAREER kicking in high gear, I was all over New Orleans, South Louisiana, and Mississippi guiding folks who wanted both a figurative and literal taste of the region. Discovering oysters was always one of the experiences I offered, simply because oysters are synonymous with Louisiana food culture and festivals.

Most people might really be intrigued to know that oysters aren't actually out in the Gulf, at least not the ones we love to eat here in Louisiana. These bivalves are in "beds" that are tended to in brackish waters. The oysters are literally farmed, and this allows them to thrive and cultivate a beautiful salty flavor. The fresh waters from the bays flushing through the oyster beds contribute to the bright flavors that are prized in South Louisiana oysters.

Oysters are harvested by boats with nets or large metal scoops dropped on either side of the vessel and then pulled through the beds, lifting up the oysters to the deck for inspection. The workers on the boat check the harvest for size. The little ones are returned to the bed with a quick toss back over the side of the boat. Once returned to the bed, they will continue to grow. The big ones are packed in sacks and are in the city by the afternoon.

The taste of an oyster, in my opinion, is almost indescribable to someone who has never experienced one. But, since you asked me, I'll be as poetic as possible. An oyster tastes salty, crisp, soft, and velvety. An oyster is smooth. It's like the bayou and the sun. An oyster tastes like Louisiana.

KEVIN'S TAKE
Two things about oysters—and I rarely eat an oyster without thinking of these two things—it's alive and Miss Yvonne.

That oyster is alive until its cut from the shell. That's why such care is taken to keep the fresh oysters cool and iced down until they are ready to be prepared for food.

Miss Yvonne Blount, my dear friend and the proprietress of Antoine's Restaurant, the 175-year-old culinary landmark in the French Quarter, is the keeper of the secret recipe, Oysters Rockefeller, created by her Grandfather Jules when there was an escargot shortage. This dish was incredibly rich, and thus he named it after the wealthiest man in the United States at that time, John D. Rockefeller. Miss Yvonne has kept the standards and legend alive as her life's mission—preserving our culinary heritage out of respect and family pride.

GARLIC OYSTERS

Serves 4

1 cup butter, divided

¼ cup garlic sauce

3 tablespoons minced garlic

¼ cup chopped parsley

½ teaspoon salt, plus extra

Vegetable oil, for frying

2 cups finely ground cornmeal

2 tablespoons Creole seasoning

1 teaspoon freshly cracked pepper, plus extra

1 large egg

½ cup milk

24 freshly shucked oysters, reserving shells

½ cup freshly grated Parmesan cheese

Green onions, sliced, for garnish

Place half the butter in a small saucepan over low to medium heat. Add garlic sauce, garlic, parsley, and salt. Cook for 5 minutes. Add remaining butter, cooking for additional 2 minutes. Remove from heat.

Heat oil in deep fryer to 375 degrees.

In a medium bowl, combine cornmeal, Creole seasoning, and pepper. In a separate bowl, whisk egg and milk together and season with salt and pepper, to taste.

Right before frying, dip each oyster in egg wash, roll in cornmeal, dip in egg wash again, then in cornmeal and immediately place in fryer. Fry until golden brown, about 2 minutes. Drain on paper towels.

Place oysters back on shells and spoon a teaspoon of garlic butter over the oysters. Top with a pinch of Parmesan and green onion.

OYSTER CHOWDER

Serves 4 to 6

---

3 cups chicken stock

1 pound golden potatoes,
cut into 1/2-inch pieces

2 tablespoons butter

3 slices bacon, finely chopped

2 cups chopped onions

1 cup chopped celery

2 cloves garlic, minced

1 bay leaf

1 tablespoon Creole seasoning

1/4 cup all-purpose flour

2 to 3 dozen oysters,
reserved in their liquid

1 1/4 cups half-and-half

1 teaspoon hot sauce

1 teaspoon salt

Parsley, for garnish

Bring stock and potatoes to boil in large, heavy saucepan over high heat. Reduce heat to medium low. Cover and simmer until potatoes are tender, about 10 minutes. Remove from heat, reserving liquid.

Melt butter in large, heavy pot over medium heat. Add bacon and cook until bacon begins to brown, about 8 minutes. Add onions, celery, garlic, bay leaf, and Creole seasoning. Sauté until vegetables soften, about 6 minutes. Stir in flour and cook 2 minutes. Gradually whisk in liquid from potatoes. Add potatoes, oysters with their liquid, half-and-half, and hot sauce. Simmer chowder 5 minutes to blend flavors, stirring frequently. Season with salt. Garnish with parsley and serve.

OYSTER TAMALES
WITH RED CHILE SAUCE

Serves 4 to 6

---

24 dried corn husks

3/4 cup shortening

6 cups masa harina

1 1/2 teaspoons baking powder

2 teaspoons salt

6 cups chicken broth

24 oysters

Red Chile Sauce (page 40)

Soak corn husks in warm water for at least 20 minutes; rinse to remove any corn silk and drain well.

To make masa, beat shortening on medium speed in a large bowl for 1 minute. In a separate bowl, stir together masa harina, baking powder, and salt.

Alternately add masa harina mixture and broth to shortening, beating well after each addition. Add just enough broth to make a thick, creamy paste.

To assemble each tamale, spread 2 tablespoons of the masa mixture on the center of the corn husk (each husk should be about 8 inches long and 6 inches wide at the top. If husks are small, overlap 2 small ones to form 1 husk of the correct size. If it is larger, tear a strip from the side). Place 1 oyster in the middle of the masa. Fold in sides of husk and fold up the bottom.

Place a mound of extra husks or a foil ball in the center of a steamer basket placed in a Dutch oven.

Lean the tamales in the basket, open side up. Add water to Dutch oven just below the basket. Bring water to boil and reduce heat. Cover and steam 40 minutes, adding water when necessary. Serve with Red Chile Sauce.

continued

RED CHILE SAUCE

15 large dried chiles (such as Anaheim, New Mexico, California, or pasilla)

5 cloves garlic

2 teaspoons ground cumin

1 teaspoon salt

2 teaspoons all-purpose flour

2 teaspoons olive oil

Preheat oven to 350 degrees.

Remove stems and seeds from dried chile peppers, and place peppers in a single layer on a baking sheet. Roast for 2–5 minutes or until you smell the roasted peppers, checking often to avoid burning. Remove from oven and soak in enough hot water to cover for about 30 minutes or until cool.

Put peppers and 2½ cups of the soaking water into a blender (save the remaining soaking water). Add garlic, cumin, and salt. Blend until smooth.

In a 2-quart saucepan, stir flour into oil over medium heat until browned. Carefully stir in chile mixture. Simmer, uncovered, for 5–10 minutes or until slightly thickened. (If sauce gets too thick, stir in up to 1 cup of the remaining soaking water until you reach the desired thickness.)

Note: When working with chiles, use rubber gloves to protect your skin and avoid contact with your eyes. Wash hands thoroughly with soap and water to remove the chile oils.

CREOLE TOMATO

EVERY MARCH, I LINE my kitchen window sill with ripening Creole tomatoes. It's an annual ritual for me that was passed down by my mother. Springtime was the beginning of the seasonal celebration of Creole tomatoes. Even before the ripe red fruit appeared at the grocery store or on the neighborhood vegetable man's truck offerings, Mom would bring the grassy green, unripened Creoles home for one of her specialties, fried green tomatoes. Uncooked, the green tomatoes are hard and tasteless. But under my mother's direction, she turned those green slices into a breaded delight.

Years later, I've never been through a season without my own bounty of locally grown Creole tomatoes. A perk of doing the cooking demonstrations at the Creole Tomato Fest is leaving with a flat of Creoles. As a matter of fact, one of my favorite yearly events is cooking on the demonstration stage at the Creole Tomato Festival at the Historic French Market. Some folks say, "Chef Kevin, really tomato pie?" And after a taste, they say, "Chef Kevin, I really love tomato pie. Can I have another taste?" Yep. New Orleans celebrates food like no other place on the planet.

For those unfamiliar, to qualify as an authentic Creole tomato, the fruit has to be grown in South Louisiana, usually in Plaquemines parish, and some consider that the Creoles must be the first tomatoes of the season. There really isn't a named variety of a tomato known as a Creole. It's more about the place and the intense flavor from the soil where they are grown. A Creole tomato tends to be on the bigger side and the depth of flavor is true.

Kevin's Take

Farmers' market growers are really special folks. They harvest right before market, bringing us shoppers' access to the freshest produce and with the most authentic flavors. We have great markets all over the city, and across Lake Pontchartrain on the North Shore, too. They are like mini festivals during growing season, which is pretty long in South Louisiana, if not year-round.

Once you become a regular at a market, you'll be very excited to know that you can actually ask the growers to harvest specific items for you. They have all kinds of tricks and recommendations. You'll be glad you took the time to cultivate a rapport with a grower.

TOMATO PIE

Serves 6 to 8

---

4 large tomatoes,
  peeled and sliced

1 teaspoon salt

12 puff pastry squares

10 fresh basil leaves, chopped

½ cup sliced green onion

1 tablespoon Creole seasoning

1 cup grated mozzarella cheese

1 cup grated cheddar cheese

1 cup mayonnaise

Preheat oven to 350 degrees. Prepare the cups of a 12-cup muffin tin with nonstick cooking spray.

Place the tomatoes in 1 layer in a colander set in the sink. Sprinkle with salt and allow to drain for 10 minutes. Line prepared muffin tins with puff pastry.

Layer the tomato slices, basil, and green onion in puff pastry. Season with Creole seasoning.

Combine the cheeses and mayonnaise together. Spread mixture on top of the tomatoes and bake for 30 minutes or until lightly browned.

Note: For a fun festival feel, use disposable foil ramekins rather than a muffin tin to make the pies.

MARGHERITA CRÊPES

Makes 8 crêpes

CRÊPES

½ cup cold milk

½ cup water, preferably cold but can be at room temperature

2 eggs, preferably cold but can be at room temperature

2 tablespoons melted butter

¾ cup sifted all-purpose flour

1 teaspoon sugar

½ teaspoon salt

FILLING

1 tablespoon Creole seasoning

1 teaspoon Italian seasoning

1 teaspoon garlic powder

Olive oil

6 plum tomatoes, sliced

1 cup chopped fresh basil

2 cups grated mozzarella cheese

CRÊPES In a mixing bowl, whisk milk, water, eggs, and butter together. In a separate large mixing bowl, whisk flour, sugar, and salt together. Slowly pour the wet ingredients into the dry ingredients, whisking constantly until everything is incorporated. Strain the batter and use a spoon to press down on the lumps against the sieve to incorporate them back into the batter. Strain the batter again and discard any remaining lumps.

Cover the batter with plastic wrap, place in the refrigerator, and chill for at least 2 hours. The batter can be made the day before and kept chilled until ready to use. The batter should be the consistency of a light cream, just thick enough to coat a spoon. If you find the batter too thick, whisk in water, 1 tablespoon at a time.

Heat a 10- to 12-inch frying pan over medium heat. Sprinkle droplets of water onto the pan and if the water sizzles immediately, it means the pan is hot enough for use. Brush a thin layer of softened or melted butter on the frying pan. Give the batter a stir and scoop ¼ cup of batter.

Pour the batter into the middle of the pan, tilting the pan in all directions as you pour so that the batter coats the bottom in a thin layer (the batter should set almost immediately as you pour it in). Cook for about 30 seconds until the edges begin to brown then loosen the crêpe with a spatula and turn to the other side to cook for another 30 seconds. Transfer the cooked crêpe to a plate.

After cooking the first crêpe, determine if ¼ cup of batter is too much or too little and adjust the batter amount for the subsequent crêpes.

FILLING Mix Creole seasoning, Italian seasoning, and garlic powder together in a small bowl.

Brush each crêpe with olive oil, add slices of tomato, and a pinch of seasoning mix. Add a sprinkle of basil and ¼ cup mozzarella cheese. Fold over and serve.

STUFFED TOMATOES
WITH GULF TUNA SALAD

Serves 4

---

2 (4- to 6-ounce) tuna steaks

1 cup orange juice

2 tablespoons olive oil

1/2 teaspoon salt

1/3 cup mayonnaise

1/4 cup finely chopped celery

1/4 cup chopped black olives

2 tablespoons finely chopped red onions

2 tablespoons chopped fresh cilantro

Zest and juice from 1/2 lemon

1 tablespoon Creole seasoning

4 large tomatoes

Parsley, for garnish

Lemon wedges

Place tuna in a shallow dish and pour orange juice over the top. Cover and refrigerate for 30 minutes.

Add olive oil to a skillet set over medium heat. Season tuna with salt and cook for 2 minutes per side. Remove tuna to rest.

In a bowl, combine mayonnaise, celery, olives, red onion, cilantro, lemon zest and juice, and Creole seasoning. Mix well. Cut tuna into cubes and add. Stir combine.

Use a serrated knife to partially cut tomatoes into wedges, starting at the top of each tomato and being careful to not cut through to bottom. Fill tomatoes with tuna mixture and garnish with parsley and lemon wedges.

GUMBO

GUMBO RECIPES ARE LIKE FINGERPRINTS. No two are exactly alike. The dark, rich Belton-Thomas roux that defined my family's gumbo heritage showed up at almost every extended relative's celebration and festivity. And I dare say gumbo appears at almost all of the festivals in the entire state of Louisiana.

I'd like to go on record here to say with conviction, "No roux, no gumbo." You can quote me on that. There is no such thing as a roux-less gumbo. That's just a soup.

My personal gumbo starts with a dark roux. It's the primer for my entire dish. Close your eyes and imagine a dark roux in terms of a cup of coffee. Dark. Toasted. Rich. Coffee, right? But it's the same for a dark roux. Those unexpected flavors are brought out by the long task of cooking the flour in oil. If you don't get your roux dark, you miss out on the rich, deep toasted flavor.

The roux is also the conduit for layering of flavors. I've never wavered in my gumbo cooking process. I cook my roux to a dark chocolate color and then I add the trinity—onions, celery, and bell peppers—and let them cook in the roux. The act of shocking the vegetables in the hot roux actually accelerates the caramelization process and allows the natural sweetness and flavors to release. After a couple of minutes, I add the seasonings and garlic and let those flavors open up. Then I ladle in the stock. And that's the base for those seasonal ingredients.

It all boils down to who is at the end of the cooking spoon. I love that everyone's gumbo is different. It should be. That difference reflects culture, and also ensures the ongoing evolution of Louisiana cuisine.

KEVIN'S TAKE Gumbo is translated from the West African words *kingombo* or *quingombo*, literally meaning okra. It's the okra originally native to Africa and brought to Louisiana by slaves that was used to thicken our now signature regional dish. These days gumbo doesn't have to have okra to be gumbo. Filé powder, ground sassafras leaves, was a New World substitute for thickening the dish. Surprisingly, the word for filé in the Choctaw language is *kombo*. Looks and sounds familiar. That's just serendipity.

GUMBO BASE

Serves 8 to 12

---

3 cups diced onions

1 cup diced celery

1 cup diced green bell pepper

1 cup sliced green onions

1 cup vegetable oil

1 cup all-purpose flour

1 tablespoon chopped garlic

2 tablespoons Creole seasoning

8 cups chicken stock

Place onions, celery, bell pepper, and green onions in a stock pot and set aside.

In a stainless steel or cast iron pan, heat oil over medium-high heat. Add flour, and use a whisk to slowly stir, making sure to cover the entire bottom of the pan until flour is a chocolate color. Pour roux on top of vegetables in stock pot and stir. Place pot over medium heat, add garlic and Creole seasoning, and stir for 2 minutes. Add stock and bring to a boil. Use this as the base for gumbo recipes of choice.

OKRA GUMBO

Serves 8 to 12

1½ pounds andouille sausage, cut in half and sliced

1 pound okra, sliced

1 recipe Gumbo Base

2 pounds shrimp, peeled and deveined

Cooked rice, to serve

Add andouille sausage and okra to a stock pot of hot Gumbo Base, and simmer for 20 minutes on medium heat. Add shrimp and cook for additional 10 minutes. Serve over rice.

GUMBO Z'HERBES

Serves 12 to 16

---

1 bunch mustard greens

1 bunch collard greens

1 bunch turnip greens

1 bunch spinach

1 head green cabbage

1 bunch kale

1 bunch Swiss chard

1 bunch carrot tops

1 bunch beet tops

1 bunch watercress

1 gallon chicken stock

1 bunch green onions, sliced

4 cups chopped onions

6 cloves garlic, minced

1 pound ham, cubed

1 pound pickled meat (or 1 additional pound ham), cubed

½ pound hot sausage

½ cup flour

1 tablespoon Creole seasoning

1 tablespoon thyme leaves

1 teaspoon cayenne pepper

1 tablespoon filé powder

Hot rice, to serve

Wash greens thoroughly to remove dirt and grit. Chop the greens and place them in a 12-quart stock pot with stock, onions, and garlic. Bring to a boil and reduce to simmer; cook, covered, for 30 minutes. Strain greens, reserving the liquid, and keep at least 2 cups stock remaining in the pot.

Add ham and pickled meat to pot and cook for 15 minutes. Take greens and place them into a food processor and pulse for a fine chop.

Remove hot sausage from casing, making small balls, and cook in a skillet to render the fat. Once cooked, add sausage to stock pot. Add flour to the rendered fat in the skillet to make a roux. Cook roux to a peanut butter color and add to stock pot and stir.

Return greens to the stock pot along with the reserved stock. Add Creole seasoning, thyme, and cayenne pepper and stir well. Reduce heat and simmer for 45 minutes. Stir in filé and serve over rice.

FILÉ GUMBO LASAGNA

Serves 8 to 12

1 pound smoked sausage, sliced

1 pound crabmeat

2 pounds shrimp, peeled and deveined

1 tablespoon salt

1 to 2 tablespoons filé powder

1 recipe Gumbo Base (page 48)

1½ to 2 pounds no-boil lasagna noodles

½ cup grated Gruyère cheese

Preheat oven to 350 degrees.

Combine sausage, crab, and shrimp in a bowl, season with salt, and mix well.

Add filé to hot Gumbo Base in a stock pot, stirring well.

Ladle ½ cup of the Gumbo Base mixture into the bottom of a 9 x 13-inch baking dish. Add a layer of noodles. Top with some of the sausage mixture and ladle ½ cup of Gumbo Base on top. Continue layering noodles, sausage mixture, and base until you lay down the top layer of noodles. Spread with remaining sausage mixture, top with cheese, and drizzle with a bit of the Gumbo Base.

Cover tightly with aluminum foil and bake for 45 minutes. Remove foil and continue to bake about 20 minutes. Remove from oven and let rest for 5–10 minutes before serving.

CRAWFISH

CRAWFISH SEASON IN SOUTH LOUISIANA runs from around February through June. The bright red crustaceans' appearance lets you know that spring is coming, and that's always something to celebrate.

Dad's late winter through springtime ritual would consist of running by my grandparents' house in the 7th Ward for a visit, and before heading home, stopping by one of the famous seafood houses on Broad Street. He didn't stop just because of marching orders delivered by Mom and Nan. He stopped because he absolutely loved crawfish and every dish Mom made with them.

Once Dad got home with the crawfish, the kitchen took on a festive atmosphere. The kitchen table was covered in *The Times Picayune* newspapers, and Dad discharged the piping hot crawfish from the lined paper sack onto the center of the table. This dinnertime ritual brought the four of us together to chat and peel crawfish. Mom boiled her own potatoes and corn to add to the bounty. All the extra crawfish, piled high and glowing bright red, was beautiful.

Once we had our fill of tail meat, the effort would switch to picking meat for Mom's crawfish creations later on in the week. It was all about getting enough tail meat for crawfish étouffée. Toward the end of the season, the sense of urgency quickened and the freezer began to fill with neatly sorted frozen bags of tail meat and cleaned shells. The last bits reserved for Thanksgiving Day's celebration, which always featured Mom's crawfish bisque with stuffed heads.

The crawfish boil party season really starts to kick in around April. Easter crawfish boils are traditional. Usually the weekend after Easter, Sid and Dawn Goodreaux host a big crawfish boil on the Northshore across Lake Pontchartrain. What started off as a few friends getting together now has teams of friends competing for the title of who boils better. It's a total "my boil is better than your boil" extravaganza. Everybody brings their pots and does their own thing. It's an incredible celebration. It's one of the greatest invitations I receive every year. This year, after so many years of being too busy to attend, I put it on my calendar and showed up on Easter Sunday. Yes. A week early and nobody was home! But, I'll be there the next time.

KEVIN'S TAKE
You can find Louisiana crawfish in most seafood sections of your grocery store year-round. These frozen packages with the orangey-looking fat are packed full of flavor. It's the fat from the meat that gives that sweet taste to your dish. Use the fat. It's where the flavor is found.

CRAWFISH ENCHILADAS
CON QUESO

Serves 8 to 10

---

8 tablespoons butter, divided

1 cup finely chopped onions

1 cup chopped canned green chiles

3/4 cup finely chopped
   green bell pepper

2 tablespoons Creole
   seasoning, divided

1 teaspoon salt

1 teaspoon minced garlic

3 cups heavy cream

1 cup sour cream

8 cups grated Monterey
   Jack cheese, divided

2 pounds peeled crawfish tails

2/3 cup very finely chopped
   green onions

20 (6-inch) corn tortillas

Preheat oven to 350 degrees.

In a large skillet, melt 4 tablespoons butter. Add the onions, green chiles, bell pepper, 1 tablespoon Creole seasoning, salt, and garlic. Sauté over medium heat for 10 minutes, stirring often. Stir in the cream and bring mixture to a rapid boil then reduce the heat and simmer, uncovered, for 10 minutes, stirring constantly. Add the sour cream and stir continuously until the sour cream has dissolved, about 3 minutes. Add 3 cups of the cheese and stir until melted. Set the sauce aside.

In a saucepan, melt the remaining butter. Add the crawfish, green onions, and the remaining Creole seasoning. Sauté over medium heat for about 6 minutes, stirring occasionally. Add the cheese sauce to the crawfish mixture and stir well. Simmer until the flavors are well-blended, 6–10 minutes, stirring occasionally. Set aside.

In a skillet, warm each tortilla for about 15 seconds on each side. Spoon about 1/3 cup of the crawfish cheese mixture on each tortilla and then roll up tortilla. Place seam side down in a baking dish. Cover the tortillas from end to end with a generous amount of additional crawfish cheese sauce. Then sprinkle with remaining cheese. Bake the enchiladas until cheese melts, 5–8 minutes. Serve immediately.

CRAWFISH-STUFFED MUSHROOMS

Serves 4

---

4 to 6 portobello mushroom caps

2 tablespoons butter

1 cup chopped onion

1/2 cup chopped celery

1/2 cup chopped red bell pepper

3 cloves garlic, minced

2 tablespoons Creole seasoning

1 teaspoon salt

1/2 teaspoon black pepper

1/2 cup grated Parmesan cheese, divided

1/2 cup grated mozzarella cheese

1 tablespoon fresh lemon juice

2 teaspoons Worcestershire sauce

2 eggs, lightly beaten

1/2 cup seasoned breadcrumbs, divided

1 pound crawfish tails, chopped

2 tablespoons chopped fresh parsley

Preheat oven to 350 degrees. Line a rimmed baking sheet with aluminum foil and spray with nonstick cooking spray.

Using a dry paper towel, lightly brush excess dirt from outside of mushroom caps. Remove and discard stems. Using a metal spoon, scrape gills and discard.

In a large skillet, melt butter over medium heat. Cook onion and celery until translucent and soft, 10–12 minutes. Add bell pepper and cook 4–6 minutes. Add garlic, Creole seasoning, salt, and pepper and cook just until fragrant, about 1 minute.

Transfer onion mixture to a large bowl, and add 1/4 cup Parmesan, mozzarella, lemon juice, Worcestershire, eggs, 1/4 cup breadcrumbs, and crawfish. Mix to combine well. Divide mixture evenly among mushroom caps and press in firmly. Top mushroom caps with remaining breadcrumbs, remaining Parmesan, and parsley. Place on prepared baking sheet and bake until lightly browned, 15–17 minutes.

CRAWFISH BALLS

Serves 4 to 6

1 pound crawfish tails

2 teaspoons salt, divided

1 large onion

4 cloves garlic, crushed

2 eggs, beaten

1 tablespoon Worcestershire sauce

1 teaspoon freshly
  squeezed lemon juice

1 teaspoon hot sauce

¼ cup chopped parsley

½ cup sliced green onions

1½ cups Italian breadcrumbs

2 tablespoons Creole seasoning

2 cups all-purpose flour

Oil, for frying

Place crawfish in a food processor with
1 teaspoon of salt. Chop the crawfish up into
pieces, being careful not to make the crawfish
mushy; they should be chunky. Place in a
large bowl.

Chop onion and garlic with remaining salt
in food processor. Add to bowl with crawfish
and stir to combine. Add eggs, Worcestershire
sauce, lemon juice, hot sauce, parsley, green
onions, and breadcrumbs. Mix ingredients well.

Shape crawfish mixture into balls.

Stir Creole seasoning into the flour and roll
balls in flour. Heat cooking oil in deep fryer
to 375 degrees. Fry 3 to 4 balls at a time in
deep fryer until brown. Drain on paper towels.
Sprinkle with salt and serve with Cocktail Sauce.

COCKTAIL SAUCE

2 cups ketchup

1 tablespoon Worcestershire sauce

1 tablespoon lemon juice

½ teaspoon olive oil

1 to 2 teaspoons horseradish

Mix all ingredients together and refrigerate
until ready to serve.

BOUDIN

BOUDIN IS ONE OF THOSE DISHES that is such a large part of Louisiana's history and culture. It is a classic Cajun rice dish stuffed into a sausage casing flavored with spices and trimmings, or what is known as the discarded pieces or "awfuls." That's the liver and other entrails from the animal that are full of flavor. The casing comes from the intestines of the animal. It's a classic-style boucherie dish rooted in French sausage making techniques.

Years ago I took my oldest son Kevin to settle in as a freshman at University of Louisiana at Lafayette. That's the heart of Cajun country. And from my travels, I knew that there were a few places he was going to need directions to. It was mostly so he could know the way to the best boudin makers. That way when he came home on the weekends, he could restock my fridge.

I set him up in his dorm room. And I suggested we head a few miles out to Scott, Louisiana. I had something I wanted him to try. We headed straight to The Best Stop Supermarket. That's where I introduced Kevin to boudin and cracklins. I really wanted him to have a little bit in the dorm room so he could heat it up and eat on the go. We bought the fresh cracklins, too. I must admit he was slightly skeptical.

This was Kevin's first time to have fresh cracklins. About a quarter of a mile down the road on the way back to the dorm, he pulled over on the shoulder and reached into the backseat and grabbed the bag of cracklins. I could tell he was hooked. Like father, like son.

It's not a celebration of the minds and appetites when I visit Kevin these days unless we make a run to pick up some boudin. Kevin's son, Carter, was two years old during one my visits. Kevin and I had just returned from our boudin run and we were hanging out in the front yard eating boudin and chatting. Carter walked up to me, and without thinking about it, I gave him a little piece of boudin. It was a tiny taste. Two minutes later he walked back up with his hand out. Both Kevin and I, father and grandfather, introduced the next generation of Belton kids to boudin and Louisiana food culture. It's a simple pleasure that is incredibly meaningful and something to celebrate.

Kevin's Take
You can buy pork skins and cracklins in the grocery store. And they are both certainly delicious. The difference is very simple. Fried or baked pork skins are just the skin and no fat at all. Cracklins are the skin with a little fat and a tiny shard of meat.

HOMEMADE BOUDIN

Makes 16 cups

---

3 cups short-grain rice, cooked and cooled

2 pounds pork shoulder, cut into 1-inch cubes

1 pound pork liver, cleaned and cut into large chunks

2 quarts chicken stock

1½ cups coarsely chopped onions

½ cup coarsely chopped green bell pepper

½ cup coarsely chopped celery

2 whole cloves garlic

2 teaspoons salt, divided

2 tablespoons Creole seasoning, divided

2 teaspoons cayenne pepper, divided

1¼ teaspoons black pepper, divided

1 cup chopped fresh parsley leaves, divided

1 cup sliced green onion, divided

Place rice in a large bowl and fluff with a fork.

In a large Dutch oven, combine pork, liver, stock, onions, bell pepper, celery, garlic, 1 teaspoon salt, 1 tablespoon Creole seasoning, ¼ teaspoon cayenne, and ½ teaspoon black pepper. Bring to a boil over high heat, reduce heat to medium low, and simmer, uncovered, until pork and liver are tender, about 1½ hours. Remove from heat and drain, reserving 1½ cups of broth.

In a meat grinder fitted with a ¼-inch dye, grind pork and liver with ¼ cup parsley and ¼ cup green onion. (The pork and liver can also be coarsely chopped, in batches, in the bowl of a food processor.)

Add the pork mixture to the rice and combine. Stir in remaining salt, Creole seasoning, cayenne, black pepper, parsley, and green onion. Mix well. Add reserved broth, about ½ cup at a time, combining until mixture is moist but holds together when squeezed.

Boudin can be stored in an airtight container for 1 week in the refrigerator or 3 months in the freezer.

FRIED BOUDIN BALLS

Makes 12 balls

1 cup all-purpose flour
  (or more, if needed)

1 cup corn flour

2 large eggs, lightly beaten

½ teaspoon salt

¼ teaspoon cayenne pepper

¼ teaspoon hot sauce

4 cups Homemade Boudin
  (page 60)

Vegetable oil, for deep frying

Combine flour and corn flour in a bowl. In another bowl, combine eggs, salt, cayenne, and hot sauce.

Form boudin into 1½-inch balls.

In a large Dutch oven, pour oil to a depth of 2 inches; heat over medium heat until a deep-fry thermometer registers 375 degrees.

Add balls, in batches, to the egg mixture then roll in the flour mixture, coating them evenly. Fry balls in small batches until light brown, 2–3 minutes. Drain on paper towels. Serve warm.

Variation: Small cubes of cheese can be added to the center of the boudin balls before coating and frying.

BOUDIN WRAPS

Makes 12 wraps

2 cups Homemade Boudin
  (page 60)

12 egg roll wrappers

Vegetable oil, for deep frying

Place 1 teaspoon of boudin in center of each egg roll wrapper. Brush wrapper edges with water and roll to seal.

In a large Dutch oven, pour oil to a depth of 2 inches; heat over medium heat until a deep-fry thermometer registers 375 degrees.

Fry wraps in batches for 2–3 minutes. Drain on paper towels. Serve warm.

BOUDIN PIZZA

Serves 4

Prepared pizza dough

¼ cup olive oil

¼ teaspoon salt

4 cloves garlic, thinly sliced

½ cup Creole mustard

¼ cup cane syrup, plus extra

1 cup thinly sliced onion

1 cup grated mozzarella cheese

1 cup sliced green onion

1 tablespoon Creole seasoning

2 cups Homemade Boudin (page 60)

Cane syrup, for drizzling

Preheat oven to 450 degrees.

Roll out pizza dough to a 14-inch circle, brush with olive oil, and sprinkle with salt. In a small bowl, mix garlic, Creole mustard, and cane syrup. Mix well and spread over dough.

Cover dough with onions, mozzarella, green onion, and Creole seasoning. Place 1-inch pinches of boudin over the top and bake for 15–20 minutes until golden brown and cheese melts. Place pizza on cooling rack to keep crust crisp. Drizzle with a thin stream of cane syrup and serve.

THE SWEET STRAWBERRY

IT'S SAID THAT THERE IS NO BETTER STRAWBERRY in the world than a Ponchatoula strawberry from Louisiana. I'd have to agree. Strawberry season in Louisiana can be a blip on the calendar, so I rush to get them as soon as I hear the crop is ready. A Louisiana strawberry is meatier and more flavorful than any other strawberry I've tasted. The delicate berries are field harvested in Tangipahoa Parish, near the town of Ponchatoula. And Ponchatoula is famous for its annual Strawberry Festival.

The Strawberry Festival takes place in the heart of downtown Ponchatoula where food booths offer strawberries in everything from cakes to pies to even fried strawberries. It's one of my favorite festivals of the year, and is just a one hour drive from New Orleans.

My mom introduced me to the flavor of strawberry when she shared one of her beloved treats, Neapolitan ice cream, with me. It was the strawberry flavor of the chocolate, vanilla, and strawberry ice cream treat that I gravitated toward.

When Dad and I would head out on Highway 11 toward Slidell to go fishing, Dad would stop and pick up a few quarts of strawberries for Mom from roadside stands when the berries were in season. We'd pull over that day for strawberries because they might not be available the next week. It was this taste of local strawberries that got me hooked. And this is where my Dad taught me that everything has a season.

When we got home, Mom would immediately rinse the berries, slice them, and sprinkle with a little sugar. Covered and setting in the refrigerator, food chemistry took over and after about an hour the berry slices would be sitting in delicious juice. The berries were perfect for that pie or cake Mom was getting ready to bake. Farm to my Mom's table. That's real food.

Kevin's Take Sugaring is key to getting the juices to develop from a bowl of sliced strawberries. Simply rinse and slice and then sprinkle with a bit of sugar. Cover, chill, and in short order you'll have a juicy, chilled topping for shortcake with fresh cream. It's a simple pleasure. One I remember fondly from childhood.

RIB-EYE STEAK SALAD
WITH STRAWBERRY BALSAMIC VINAIGRETTE

Serves 4

1 rib-eye steak

Creole seasoning, to taste

1 teaspoon garlic powder

1 cup fresh green beans,
   cut into 1-inch pieces

1 head romaine lettuce, chopped

4 eggs, hard-boiled

1 pint cherry tomatoes, halved

1/2 cup pecan pieces

4 ounces crumbled blue cheese

Heat a cast iron skillet to medium-high heat.

Season steak on both sides with Creole seasoning and garlic powder. Place in skillet and cook each side for 5–6 minutes. Remove from pan and set aside to rest. Do not cut until you are ready to assemble salad.

Bring a small pot of water to a boil. Add green beans to pot and cook for 2–3 minutes on medium heat. Immediately throw green beans in an ice bath to shock them to stop the cooking process.

To assemble salad, evenly distribute lettuce, eggs, tomatoes, green beans, pecans, blue cheese, and sliced steak on 4 plates, or in Mason jars for a fun serving idea. Serve with Strawberry Balsamic Vinaigrette.

STRAWBERRY BALSAMIC VINAIGRETTE *Makes 1 cup*

1 cup strawberries, cleaned
   and green leaves removed

2 tablespoons balsamic vinegar

2 teaspoons honey

3 tablespoons extra virgin olive oil

Place strawberries, vinegar, honey, and olive oil in a blender and blend on low speed until thoroughly combined. If your strawberries are not as sweet as you prefer, adjust flavor by adding more honey.

CHOCOLATE WAFFLE BOWLS
WITH CHOCOLATE-DIPPED STRAWBERRIES

Serves 4 to 6

1³/₄ cups all-purpose flour

1/2 cup cocoa powder

2 teaspoons baking powder

1 teaspoon baking soda

1/2 cup sugar

1/4 teaspoon salt

1³/₄ cups buttermilk

1 teaspoon vanilla extract

2 eggs

6 tablespoons cooking oil

Preheat a waffle bowl maker on medium-high heat, or according to instructions for your waffle maker. Position a rack in the center of the oven and preheat to 200 degrees. Place a wire rack on a baking sheet and set aside.

In a large bowl, combine the flour, cocoa powder, baking powder, baking soda, sugar, and salt; whisk and set aside. In a large measuring cup, mix together the buttermilk, vanilla, eggs, and oil. Pour the wet ingredients into the dry ingredients and mix until combined.

Pour 1/3 to 1/2 cup of batter into each compartment of the waffle maker (the amount will depend on whether you're making large round waffles or traditional square ones). Cook the waffle for 4–6 minute or until crisp and cooked through. Transfer to the prepared baking rack and keep warm in the oven until ready to serve. Repeat with the rest of the batter. Serve filled with chocolate strawberries.

Note: If you don't have a waffle bowl maker, you can use a regular waffle iron and top the waffles with the chocolate strawberries.

CHOCOLATE-DIPPED STRAWBERRIES

1 cup semisweet chocolate chips

1/4 cup heavy cream

24 strawberries

Melt chocolate and cream together in a bowl set over simmering water until just melted. Stir and remove from heat. Dip each strawberry in chocolate and set aside on waxed or parchment paper to dry.

STRAWBERRY ICEBOX PIE

Serves 8

CRUST

14 graham cracker sheets

3/4 cup pecan pieces

1/4 cup light brown sugar

1/2 teaspoon salt

8 tablespoons butter, melted

FILLING

16 ounces frozen strawberries

1 1/4 cups heavy whipping cream

4 ounces cream cheese, room temperature

1 (14-ounce) can sweetened condensed milk

Extra whipped cream, for serving

Fresh strawberries, for serving

CRUST Combine the graham crackers, pecans, brown sugar, and salt in a food processor or blender and process until the crackers are in crumbs and everything is well-combined. Pour the crumbs into a bowl and stir in the butter to combine. Pat the mixture into the bottom of a 9-inch springform pan and set aside while you prepare the filling.

FILLING Set the strawberries out at room temperature while you prepare the whipped cream. In the bowl of a stand mixer or a large mixing bowl, use a whisk attachment to whip the cream until stiff peaks form. Set aside.

Process the frozen berries in a food processor to a thick slush. In a large bowl or the bowl of a stand mixer, cream the cream cheese and condensed milk until smooth. Beat the berries into the cream cheese mixture then fold in the whipped cream.

Pour the mixture on top of the prepared crust, cover the pan with a sheet of plastic wrap, and place on an even surface in the freezer until solid, 6 hours or overnight. Once frozen, let set at room temperature for 10 minutes prior to slicing.

Serve with additional whipped cream or fresh berries, if desired.

FLAVORFUL CATFISH

DAD AND MY UNCLE CHET always went upriver around Des Allemands to catch catfish. There is just something about Des Allemands catfish flavor. The meat is sweet and smooth as opposed to a river catfish with a much stronger flavor. Des Allemands is the place to be for catfish fishing. That's why they started the Catfish Festival in 1975. In 1980, the Louisiana legislature named Des Allemands the Catfish Capital of the Universe. My dad and Uncle Chet knew that long ago. It wasn't unusual for Uncle Chet to show up with a 30- or 40-pound catfish. That is a huge chunk of meat. He was excellent at getting those fillets cut to a perfect $1/4$-inch thickness for Mom to bread and fry.

One of the biggest catfish I've ever seen in my life was one of the few times I've seen Dad excited enough to pull the car over. We were driving on River Road along the Mississippi River around the Huey P. Long Bridge for some errand and Dad noticed a car on the levee side of the road with a huge crowd gathered around it. A man was struggling to lift a monster catfish he had caught into the trunk of his car. That catfish must have weighted at least 100 pounds.

Dad said that man was going to feed his family, his neighbors, and everybody at work. Everyone on the block probably got a little bag of catfish that day. I asked my dad about the flavor, especially since it was so big and from the Mississippi River. Dad told me the reason that fish was so big was that it was feeding on the grains that fell from the boats and granaries along the river between the levee and batture, that little piece of dry ground that pops up during low water. That fish probably tasted incredible.

KEVIN'S TAKE Catfish has a reputation as a bottom feeder and tasting earthy. And it is always a little challenging to clean. It's more head than body. So many people just think it's not worth the trouble. Not the Belton clan. Luckily, catfish fillets are the norm in the supermarket today. You can sauté, bake, or deep fry them.

POTATO CHIP-CRUSTED CATFISH NUGGETS
WITH CREOLE MAYONNAISE

Serves 4

CREOLE MAYONNAISE

3 tablespoons mayonnaise

1 teaspoon Creole mustard or coarse-grained mustard

1 teaspoon prepared horseradish

1 teaspoon hot sauce

1 teaspoon garlic sauce

CATFISH NUGGETS

16 ounces catfish fillets

2 tablespoons Creole seasoning

2 (5-ounce) bags Zapp's Salt & Vinegar potato chips or any salty kettle-style chips

1 large egg, beaten

3 tablespoons milk

1 1/2 cups all-purpose flour

Vegetable or peanut oil

1 lemon, quartered

CREOLE MAYONNAISE In a mixing bowl, combine the mayonnaise, mustard, horseradish, hot sauce, and garlic sauce. Cover and chill until ready to use.

CATFISH NUGGETS Season the catfish fillets with Creole seasoning and slice into nugget-size chunks.

Place the chips in the bowl of a food processor and pulse on high until completely pulverized to resemble breadcrumbs. Pour into a shallow bowl.

In another shallow bowl, whisk egg with the milk to make an egg wash. Place the flour in a third shallow bowl.

In a deep cast iron pot over medium-high heat, heat the oil to 375 degrees. Working in batches, coat the catfish nuggets with flour, drench in the egg wash, and then roll in the potato chips, coating evenly.

Place the nuggets in the hot oil and fry until cooked through and golden brown, about 8 minutes. Drain the catfish on a wire rack placed over a paper towel-lined platter. Serve immediately with the Creole Mayonnaise and lemon wedges.

CATFISH TACOS
WITH CHIMICHURRI SAUCE

Serves 4 to 6

TOPPINGS

Chimichurri Sauce

2 cups finely shredded
  purple cabbage

12 cherry tomatoes, halved

3 chopped tablespoons cilantro

1 avocado, sliced

1 lime cut into wedges

TACOS

2 catfish fillets

Fresh lime juice

3 tablespoons Creole seasoning

2 tablespoons extra virgin olive oil

12 (6-inch) corn tortillas

TOPPINGS Prepare all the toppings and set aside.

TACOS Pat the fish dry with paper towels and squeeze lime juice over both sides of the fillets, coating evenly. Season both sides of the fish with Creole seasoning, making sure the fillets are generously seasoned.

Heat the olive oil over medium-high heat in a skillet. Sear the fish until white and flaky on the inside and golden brown on the outside, about 5 minutes per side. Remove from pan and cut into pieces to fit into tortillas.

Heat the tortillas for 15 seconds in a warm skillet, and then assemble tacos with fish and toppings. Serve with a lime wedge.

CHIMICHURRI SAUCE

1 cup parsley leaves

4 cloves garlic

2 tablespoons oregano leaves

1/3 cup olive oil

2 tablespoons red wine vinegar

1/2 teaspoon lemon juice

1/2 teaspoon salt

1/8 teaspoon black pepper

1/4 teaspoon red pepper flakes

Finely chop parsley, garlic, and oregano in a food processor and place in a bowl. Stir in olive oil, vinegar, lemon juice, salt, pepper, and red pepper flakes. Adjust seasoning to your taste.

SMOKED CATFISH DIP

Serves 8

---

8 ounces cream cheese, softened

½ cup sour cream

½ lemon, juiced

1 tablespoon Creole seasoning

½ teaspoon dry dill weed, divided

Hot sauce, to taste

8 ounces Smoked Catfish, flaked

1 baguette, sliced and toasted

Using a blender, blend cream cheese, sour cream, lemon juice, Creole seasoning, ¼ teaspoon dill weed, and hot sauce together until thoroughly combined. Carefully fold in flaked catfish, don't over stir. Place in a serving bowl and garnish with remaining dill weed. Serve with baguette toasts.

SMOKED CATFISH

2 tablespoons salt

2 tablespoons sugar

1 tablespoon Creole seasoning

1 tablespoon garlic powder

2 cups water

16 ounces catfish fillets, cut into 4 pieces

Mix salt, sugar, Creole seasoning, garlic powder, and water in a bowl. Place catfish in a shallow dish and pour brine over the top. Cover and refrigerate for 1 hour. Pat fillets dry and smoke for 30 minutes.

If you do not have a smoker, drizzle the fillets with a little oil and season with Creole seasoning and salt. In a skillet, heat 2 tablespoons of oil over medium and sauté fish 2–3 minutes per side. Remove from pan and allow to cool slightly.

THE HAND PIE

THE RICH SOUTHERN TRADITION of sweet pies reminds me of Sunday summertime dinners at home. On the countertop, usually covered with a glass dome, was one of Mom's pies beckoning me with gooey fruit filling sitting in a freshly baked crust. Mom made apple, blueberry, strawberry, and sweet potato, but my favorite was her peach pie.

Pie is a Southern staple, particularly in the summer when all of the fruits are in season, and they come in all shapes and sizes. A full-size pie that serves eight or a single-serving fried hand pie are both part of our repertoire. I still long for a Hubig's deep-fried hand pie piping hot from the kettles on Dauphine Street. It was the hand pie of my youth. The fact that I'm longing for them more than ten years after the last pie was served is a testament to pie as a New Orleanian's true palate pleaser.

Weekends often meant that Dad would load us up in the car and take us on a drive. We'd cruise the River Road until we happened into Baton Rouge. Sometimes we'd continue up north to get a bit of the Louisiana country fresh air. I'd think of these drives like an expedition. One that usually revolved around eating along the way. In Louisiana, as you wind through the small towns, the food culture changes from place to place. I knew if we headed toward Alexandria we would end up in Lacompte and a stop at Lea's Lunchroom. Back in the 70s, Lea's made every type of sweet pie you could think of: peach, apple, strawberry, pumpkin, sweet potato. We'd always stop for pie. A perfect memory.

As you drove further north, the other side of Alexandria, and closer to Natchitoches, the pies changed personality. That's meat pie country.

We are a pie culture here in Louisiana. And even through our traditional desserts in New Orleans especially revolve around bread pudding, bananas foster, and other unique Louisiana renditions, it's the pie culture of New Orleans that captures the flavors of our rich food tradition. And, hey, we haven't even talked about peanut butter pie. See? It's endless.

Kevin's Take Practice making a good pie dough. The number one tip is to not overwork the dough. If you overwork it, it gets tough. Usually the simpler the recipe, the better your results. Once you master the dough the rest is, dare I say, easy as pie.

NATCHITOCHES MEAT PIES

Serves 8 to 12

FILLING

1 tablespoon vegetable oil

1 tablespoon butter

1/2 cup diced onion

1/2 cup diced red bell pepper

1/2 cup diced celery

1/2 cup thinly sliced green onions

1/4 cup finely chopped parsley

1 tablespoon minced garlic

1/2 pound lean ground beef

1/2 pound ground pork

Beef stock, as needed

2 tablespoons kosher salt

2 tablespoons Creole seasoning

1 tablespoon hot sauce

1 teaspoon cayenne pepper

Vegetable oil, for deep frying

DOUGH

1/2 cup vegetable shortening

2 1/2 cups all-purpose flour, divided

1 egg yolk

1/2 cup water

1 egg

1 tablespoon water

FILLING In a heavy-bottom sauté pan, heat oil and butter over medium-high heat. Add onion, bell pepper, celery, green onions, and parsley and sauté about 15 minutes or until vegetables are softened. Add the garlic for the last minute of cooking time. Add the beef and pork and sauté until cooked through and most of the liquid has reduced. Turn heat down and cook at a low simmer for about 60 minutes. Add small amounts of stock as necessary to prevent sticking. Season with salt, Creole seasoning, hot sauce, and cayenne pepper. Remove from heat and let cool.

DOUGH Cut shortening into 2 cups of flour. Stir in egg yolk and 1/2 cup water to form a sticky dough. Turn out onto a floured surface and sprinkle remaining flour on top, a little at a time, working it in until dough is smooth.

Preheat fryer to 375 degrees. Roll out the dough on a lightly floured surface and cut into 3- to 5-inch rounds. Portion out the meat mixture onto 1 side of each of the rounds. Whisk whole egg and water together for the egg wash. Brush edges of dough with egg wash then fold dough over, and using a fork, press edges to seal. Don't brush the egg wash on the tops. Fry the pies until golden brown and drain on paper towels. Serve hot.

CRAWFISH PIES

Serves 8 to 12

FILLING

1 tablespoon vegetable oil

1 tablespoon butter

1/2 cup diced onion

1/2 cup diced red bell pepper

1/2 cup diced celery

1/2 cup thinly sliced green onions

1/4 cup finely chopped parsley

1 tablespoon minced garlic

1 pound crawfish meat, finely chopped

Chicken stock, as needed

2 tablespoons kosher salt

2 tablespoons Creole seasoning

1 tablespoon hot sauce

1 teaspoon cayenne pepper

Vegetable oil, for deep frying

DOUGH

1/2 cup vegetable shortening

2 1/2 cups all-purpose flour, divided

1 egg yolk

1/2 cup water

1 egg

1 tablespoon water

FILLING In a heavy-bottom sauté pan, heat oil and butter over medium-high heat. Add onion, bell pepper, and celery and sauté about 15 minutes or until vegetables are softened. Add green onions, parsley, and garlic and sauté for 5 minutes. Add crawfish, stirring well, and cook for another 5 minutes. Add small amounts of stock as necessary to prevent sticking. Season with salt, Creole seasoning, hot sauce, and cayenne pepper. Remove from heat and let cool.

DOUGH Cut shortening into 2 cups of flour. Stir in egg yolk and 1/2 cup water to form a sticky dough. Turn out onto a floured surface and sprinkle remaining flour on top, a little at a time, working it in until dough is smooth.

Preheat fryer to 375 degrees. Roll out the dough on a lightly floured surface and cut into 3- to 5-inch rounds. Portion out the crawfish mixture onto 1 side of each of the rounds. Whisk whole egg and water together for the egg wash. Brush edges of dough with egg wash then fold dough over, and using a fork, press edges to seal. Don't brush the egg wash on the tops. Fry the pies until golden brown and drain on paper towels. Serve hot.

FRUIT HAND PIES

Serves 8 to 12

FILLING

1 (3-ounce) package dried apples, chopped

2 cups apple juice

1 tablespoon lemon juice

1/2 cup sugar

1 teaspoon cinnamon

2 tablespoons butter

DOUGH

1/2 cup vegetable shortening

2 1/2 cups all-purpose flour, divided

1 egg yolk

1/2 cup water

1 egg

1 tablespoon water

Vegetable oil, for deep frying

GLAZE

1 (14-ounce) can of condensed milk

1 cup packed light brown sugar

2 tablespoons butter

1/2 teaspoon vanilla

2 tablespoons lemon juice

FILLING In a medium saucepan, heat apples, apple juice, and lemon juice, bringing to a boil. Reduce heat and simmer on low until apples are soft and liquid is cooked off. This may take about 1 hour. If apples are not soft enough to mash, add a little more juice and cook longer. Remove from heat, mash apples with fork, and add sugar, cinnamon, and butter. Let cool.

DOUGH Cut shortening into 2 cups of flour. Stir in egg yolk and 1/2 cup water to form a sticky dough. Turn out onto a floured surface and sprinkle remaining flour on top, a little at a time, working it in until dough is smooth.

Preheat fryer to 375 degrees. Roll out the dough on a lightly floured surface and cut into 3- to 5-inch rounds. Portion out the apple mixture onto 1 side of each of the rounds. Whisk whole egg and water together for the egg wash. Brush edges of dough with egg wash then fold dough over, and using a fork, press edges to seal. Don't brush the egg wash on the tops. Fry the pies until golden brown and drain on paper towels. Serve hot.

GLAZE Combine condensed milk and brown sugar in a saucepan and simmer over medium heat. Lower heat, stirring for 5 minutes until thick. Remove from heat and stir in butter, vanilla, and lemon juice.

Spoon glaze over pies 5 minutes after they have been cooked.

JAMMIN' ON JAMBALAYA

THERE ARE TWO DIFFERENT TYPES of jambalaya: Cajun and Creole. A Cajun jambalaya is brown, taking its color from the spices, meats, and sausages used to make it. And it does not have tomatoes in it. A Creole jambalaya is red with the addition of tomato, and takes on a lighter look and flavor with seafood as the main ingredient.

What these two jambalayas have in common is definitely technique. And of course, both finished dishes must be textural. I mean you have to be able to see the ingredients. A proper jambalaya done right has every grain of rice, every slice of sausage, every piece of vegetable discernible. And the flavor has to be balanced. The rice is the star of jambalaya because it carries all of the flavor. A jambalaya can be made with any meat, seafood, or a combination of the two. I've made vegetarian versions with broccoli, cauliflower, carrots, and fresh corn off the cob. I've also used some of the soy sausages available with specialty seasonings already added. These are great for flavor in a vegetarian jambalaya. The combinations are endless.

When I arrived at LSU for my first semester of college, one of the huge cultural events I was introduced to was the college game-day tailgate party. That's where I became acquainted with jambalaya cooking the Cajun way. Big, bold, and enough to feed everybody in the neighborhood. What I saw on the night before kickoff blew me away. The parking lots on campus turned into villages of Tiger fans settling down and preparing for the big cookouts the following day. Turned out in almost every individual tailgate village, or cluster of campers, was a huge cast iron pot like a cauldron out of a nursery rhyme, and it was accompanied by a tailgate chef preparing to feed hordes of hungry football fans.

This tailgate version of traditional jambalaya is a huge undertaking. We are talking ten pounds of sausage. Eight to ten pounds of chicken meat. Onions, celery, and bell peppers by the bucket. And pounds of rice and cups of seasoning. This is a whole different cooking ballgame, and it all takes place in makeshift kitchens in a parking lot around the stadium. Add a little parking lot cooking competition, and you've got the perfect ingredients for quite a celebration and gathering.

KEVIN'S TAKE One of the nice things about jambalaya is that it is one-pot cooking. A true jambalaya is prepared using uncooked rice so all the flavors are absorbed and cooked together. But every once in a while, I like to change things up and make traditional jambalaya using pasta—Pastalaya! And all my boys LOVE it!

PASTALAYA

Serves 6 to 8

2 tablespoons olive oil

1 pound smoked sausage

1 cup diced onion

½ cup diced celery

½ cup diced green bell pepper

1 tablespoon minced garlic

2 tablespoons Creole seasoning

1 teaspoon salt

1 tablespoon red pepper flakes

1 tablespoon chopped fresh oregano

¼ cup tomato paste

1 pound thin spaghetti, broken

4 cups chicken stock

1 pound shrimp, peeled and deveined

¼ cup parsley, chopped

½ cup sliced green onions

In a Dutch oven, heat olive oil over medium heat and add sausage. Cook for 2 minutes then add onion, celery, and bell pepper, cooking for another 5 minutes. Stir in garlic, Creole seasoning, salt, red pepper flakes, and oregano. Stir in tomato paste, then after 1 minute, stir in spaghetti and mix well. Add stock, stir, and bring to a boil. Cover, reduce heat low, and cook for 10 minutes. Stir in shrimp and cook for 5 minutes. Remove from heat, and stir in parsley and green onions. Cover and let rest 5 minutes before serving.

BREAKFAST JAMBALAYA

Serves 6 to 8

---

8 bacon strips, sliced

1 tablespoon vegetable oil

4 breakfast sausage links, sliced

4 breakfast sausage patties, diced

2 cups chopped onions

1 cup chopped celery

1 cup chopped red bell pepper

2 tablespoons Creole seasoning

1 teaspoon salt

2 tablespoons minced garlic

1 teaspoon thyme

2 bay leaves

1/2 cup chopped parsley

2 tablespoons paprika

1/4 cup tomato paste

2 1/2 cups chicken stock

2 cups uncooked long-grain rice

1/2 cup sliced green onions

1 cup grated cheddar cheese

Butter, for cooking eggs

12 eggs

In a large pot, cook bacon in oil until crisp. Remove bacon, drain on paper towels, and set aside. Add sausage links and patties, onions, celery, and bell pepper to the pot. Cook for 5 minutes then add Creole seasoning, salt, garlic, thyme, bay leaves, parsley, and paprika. Stir well, add tomato paste and stock, and bring to a boil. Add rice, and bring back to a boil.

Reduce heat and simmer for 10 minutes. Remove from heat and stir thoroughly. Replace cover and let set for 15 minutes. Stir in green onions, cover, and start cooking eggs—over easy, scrambled, poached, your choice.

To serve jambalaya, sprinkle with cheese then place eggs on top.

JAMBALAYA-STUFFED CHICKEN THIGHS

Serves 6 to 8

JAMBALAYA

2 tablespoons vegetable oil

1 pound smoked sausage, sliced

2 cups chopped onions

1 cup chopped celery

1 cup chopped green bell pepper

1 tablespoon minced garlic

1 chicken thigh, diced

2 tablespoons Creole seasoning

1 teaspoon salt

2½ cups chicken stock

3 tablespoons Kitchen Bouquet

2 cups uncooked long-grain rice

¼ cup chopped parsley

CHICKEN THIGHS

12 deboned chicken
thighs with skin on

4 tablespoons Creole seasoning

2 tablespoons sour cream

2 tablespoons paprika

JAMBALAYA In a pot, heat oil over medium heat. Add sausage and cook for 2 minutes. Add onions, celery, and bell pepper and sauté for 5 minutes. Stir in garlic, chicken, Creole seasoning, and salt. Stir well, add stock and Kitchen Bouquet, and bring to a boil. Stir in rice, bring back to a boil, cover, and reduce heat to a simmer for 10 minutes. Remove from heat, stir in parsley, mixing well, cover, and let set for 15 minutes.

CHICKEN THIGHS Preheat oven to 375 degrees.

Place 1 or 2 chicken thighs, skin side down, on a piece of plastic wrap. Season each thigh with Creole seasoning. Place another piece of plastic wrap over the seasoned thighs and beat with a meat mallet until the chicken is about ¼ inch thick. Repeat with remaining thighs.

In the middle of each chicken thigh add 2 to 4 tablespoons of Jambalaya. Roll each thigh tightly, making sure to keep the rice from coming out of the sides. Place each roll in a 9 x 13-inch baking dish and brush the tops with sour cream.

Cover with aluminum foil and bake for 20–25 minutes. Make sure the foil is not touching the rolls. After 25 minutes, remove the foil. There will be excess oil and liquid in the dish. Drain out some of the oil, lightly sprinkle the tops with paprika, and bake for another 15 minutes. To check for doneness, place a thermometer in thickest part of the chicken, making sure it has reached 165 degrees internal temperature.

Serve chicken with extra Jambalaya not used for stuffing.

RICE

ONE OF THE LARGEST and most significant festivals in Louisiana is in Crowley every October. The International Rice Festival is the oldest festival to celebrate a Louisiana-grown harvest. It's been around since 1937. The festival is based in West Louisiana where the soil is perennially wet and silty from river deposits. That's perfect conditions to farm rice, where the young plants need to sit in flooded fields at the first growth stage. Rice is grown all over Louisiana, and is quite something to celebrate. I do my part everyday by eating Louisiana rice, that's for sure.

I might not have known what Mom was cooking for dinner, but no matter what she cooked, rice was going to be on the table. She boiled her rice, and stirred it with her own cadence every few minutes according to her mental timer. She would simply taste a few grains intermittently while she'd go back and forth and stir and stir then taste and taste. Once the rice was cooked the way she wanted, she would pour it out into a colander over the sink and rinse it in cold water to stop it from cooking. Then she'd rinse her pot. Next, she would add a couple of inches of water and set that pot back on the stove. The colander filled with the rice, covered with aluminum foil, would go right back on the rice pot. A few minutes before serving dinner, she'd turn the fire on and steam the rice again. Fluffy and perfect. I cook my rice the same way because it tastes better, and the texture holds for a couple of days in the refrigerator.

Rice makes everything we eat in Louisiana better, and puts a regional stamp on our dishes.

KEVIN'S TAKE When cooking rice, be careful not to overcook it. You should see each grain. There are thousands of varieties of rice, but only three types: long grain, medium grain, and short grain. The shorter the grain, the higher the starch content. Long-grain rice is perfect for a jambalaya. Medium-grain rice best for boudin, and is my preferred rice in general. We don't grow much short-grain rice in Louisiana. Leftover rice is perfect for making a sweet rice pudding, or adding a little egg and sweetened flour to make Calas, fried rice balls dusted with powdered sugar, a Creole delicacy.

BAKED RICE AU GRATIN

Serves 8 to 10

¼ cup Italian breadcrumbs

1 cup grated Parmigiano-Reggiano cheese, divided

2 tablespoons olive oil

2 cups chopped onions

1 teaspoon minced garlic

2 tablespoons flour

2 pounds portobello mushrooms, chopped

2 cups milk

¾ cup uncooked jasmine rice

1 tablespoon Creole seasoning

1 teaspoon chopped fresh thyme

1 teaspoon salt

Preheat oven to 425 degrees.

Combine breadcrumbs and ¼ cup cheese in a small bowl and set aside.

In a large skillet, heat oil over medium heat and add onions, cooking until browned, 5–7 minutes. Add garlic, cooking for 1 minute. Add flour and stir well. Stir in mushrooms, and then add milk, rice, Creole seasoning, thyme, salt, and remaining cheese; stir to combine.

Spoon mixture into a lightly buttered 9 x 9-inch baking dish. Bake until set, 35–40 minutes. Remove from oven and raise oven temperature to broil. Sprinkle top with breadcrumb mixture and place under broiler for 2–3 minutes or until golden brown.

BROCCOLI FRIED RICE

Serves 6 to 8

---

3 cups broccoli, chopped

2 tablespoons sesame oil, divided

1/2 cup chopped yellow onion

2 cloves garlic, minced

3 cups cooked and
cooled brown rice

2 teaspoons Creole seasoning

1/2 cup peas

1/2 cup diced carrots

1/4 cup soy sauce

1/2 teaspoon garlic powder

1 egg

1 teaspoon sesame seeds

1/2 cup sliced green onions

Salt and pepper, to taste

Add broccoli to a food processor. Pulse until broccoli resembles rice.

Heat a large nonstick pan to a high heat. Add 1 tablespoon sesame oil. Once the oil is hot, add onion and garlic. Stir-fry until fragrant, about 30 seconds. Add broccoli and stir-fry for 1 minute, until broccoli begins to cook. Add remaining oil and rice. Stir-fry the mixture for 2 minutes.

Add Creole seasoning, peas, carrots, soy sauce, and garlic powder. Continue to cook another 2–3 minutes until sauce has coated all the rice and veggies. Reduce the heat to medium and make a well in the center of the mixture. Crack the egg in the middle and scramble. Mix in to the rice.

Add sesame seeds and green onions. Toss and season to taste with salt and pepper. Serve hot.

BACON AND EGG CALAS

Serves 4

Vegetable oil, for frying

1 cup all-purpose flour

1¼ teaspoons baking powder

1 teaspoon Creole seasoning

½ teaspoon garlic powder

½ teaspoon cumin

3 eggs

2 teaspoons Worcestershire sauce

½ teaspoon salt

¼ cup grated cheddar cheese

1½ cups cooked rice, chilled

4 bacon strips, cooked and crumbled

¼ cup green onions, finely chopped

4 hard-boiled eggs

Flour, for dusting eggs

Heat oil to 375 degrees.

Combine flour, baking powder, Creole seasoning, garlic powder, and cumin. Sift thoroughly and set aside.

In a medium bowl, beat the eggs, Worcestershire sauce, and salt for about 2 minutes. Add cheese and about half of the dry ingredients and mix well. Add remaining dry ingredients. Add rice, bacon, and green onions to wet batter and combine until the mixture comes together.

Dust hard-boiled eggs with flour. This will allow the rice mixture to adhere to the eggs. Taking some of the rice mixture, press it around each egg, completely encasing them into balls.

Gently place the rice ball into fryer, not overcrowding. Fry for 5-7 minutes until golden brown. Use a slotted spoon to move the calas around to make sure they cook evenly. Drain on paper towels.

GREEK HERITAGE

IT'S A CONVERGENCE OF FOOD, CULTURE, and music that makes the perfect recipe for a Louisiana festival. Festival culture in Louisiana hasn't always been judged by the mega-festivals of which there are a handful, but rather by the smaller, intimate festivals that get their inspiration from cultural celebrations. Of those, church celebrations across the state are some of the oldest and most significant when it comes to bringing locals together to celebrate. The Greek Festival, created by the parishioners of the Holy Trinity Greek Orthodox Cathedral on Bayou St. John, embodies this style of festival.

The Greek Festival takes the cake, or should I say baklava, in this instance. As with many festivals, it's the unique or the hard-to-find foods and dishes presented at these annual events that become the reason people flock to the celebration. In New Orleans, the Greek Festival embodies this purpose.

I mean, it's not your grandmother's food unless your grandmother is Greek! There are trays and trays of baklava, and spiced meats roasted and carved thinly to pile high on pita bread topped with yogurt sauce. It's these special flavors that define a culture. And it is this culture that inspires Louisiana festivals year-round with people from all walks of life lining up to take in the atmosphere, and the food.

KeVin's Take Stuffed grape leaves seem so extraordinary, and I'd never really thought about making them. But, for sure, I order them most every time I see them on a menu. So when I crafted this recipe for Dolmades, I discovered a little trick that helped me keep the leaves together instead of falling apart while cooking in the pot. Get them all loaded up then set a plate on top of them. The plate needs to fit down into the pot and act as a weight. Then pour in your stock. This keeps the leaves from loosening and floating around. You can use this trick, but just make sure your plate can take the high heat. I'd avoid Mom's good china!

GREEK LENTIL SALAD

Serves 4

TZATZIKI SAUCE

½ cup cucumber, peeled, seeded, and grated

½ cup Greek yogurt

1 tablespoon lemon juice

2 teaspoons chopped fresh dill

¼ teaspoon salt

1 clove garlic, minced

SALAD

1 cup dry black beluga lentils

3 cups chicken stock

3 cups chopped baby spinach

½ cup chopped red onion

⅓ cup chopped sun-dried tomatoes

⅓ cup pitted and chopped kalamata olives

⅓ cup chopped basil

Salt and pepper, to taste

Crumbled feta cheese, for garnish

TZATZIKI SAUCE Combine all ingredients and lightly process in a blender to a smooth consistency. Cover and chill.

SALAD Pick through the lentils and remove any debris. Pour the lentils into a fine-mesh colander and rinse under running water then put into a medium saucepan. Add the stock and bring the mixture to a boil over medium-high heat.

Reduce heat to maintain a simmer and cook, stirring occasionally, until the lentils are tender, 25–35 minutes. Then drain the lentils and return them to the pan to cool for about 5 minutes.

Meanwhile, in a medium serving bowl, combine the spinach, red onion, sun-dried tomatoes, olives, and basil. Add the lentils to the serving bowl. Pour Tzatziki Sauce over the salad and toss until combined. Taste and season with salt and pepper. Sprinkle with feta and serve.

GRILLED SHRIMP GYROS
WITH HERBED YOGURT SPREAD

Serves 4

2 tablespoons Greek seasoning

2 tablespoons olive oil

1½ pounds shrimp, peeled and deveined

6 (12-inch) wooden skewers, soaked

4 (8-inch) pita rounds or gyro rounds

Herbed Yogurt Spread

½ cup crumbled feta cheese

1 large tomato, chopped

1 cucumber, thinly sliced

Preheat oven to 350 degrees.

Combine seasoning and olive oil in a heavy-duty ziptop plastic bag; add shrimp. Seal and chill 30 minutes. Soak skewers in water 30 minutes while shrimp marinates.

Thread shrimp onto skewers. Grill, covered with lid, over medium heat (300–350 degrees) for about 5 minutes on each side, or just until shrimp turn pink. You can also cook the shrimp in a cast iron pan instead of a grill.

Wrap pita rounds in aluminum foil and place in oven for 10–15 minutes to warm. When warm, spread the inside of each pita with Herbed Yogurt. Evenly add the shrimp, cheese, tomato, and cucumber to the pita pockets and serve with additional spread.

HERBED YOGURT SPREAD

2 cups Greek yogurt

3 tablespoons finely chopped parsley

3 tablespoons finely chopped mint

1 tablespoon finely chopped dill

2 cloves garlic, minced

1 tablespoon lemon zest

1 tablespoon lemon juice

Salt, to taste

Combine all ingredients and mix well. Place in refrigerate to chill until ready to use.

DOLMADES

Serves 4 to 6

---

1 (8-ounce) jar grape leaves (about 25 leaves)

1 pound ground round

1 pound ground lamb

2 tablespoons Creole seasoning

1 tablespoon salt

1 tablespoon minced fresh parsley

1 box tabbouleh mix

1 onion, finely chopped

1 clove garlic, minced

6 cups chicken stock

4 eggs

4 lemons, juiced

Drain, rinse, and dry grape leaves; set side.

In a large bowl, combine ground round, lamb, Creole seasoning, salt, parsley, tabbouleh, onion, and garlic and mix well.

Lay out 1 grape leaf, stem up, and place about 1 rounded tablespoon meat mixture near stem.

Fold the stem over meat mixture, fold 1 side of the leaf over mixture, fold top over, then roll the rest, but not too tightly. Repeat, using all of the leaves. Use toothpicks to keep the stuffed leaves together. Snuggly place rolls in a large pot. If you have extra meat mixture, you can roll it into small balls and place in pot.

Place a heat-proof plate on top of the stuffed leaves, and pour in the stock, adding water if you need to. Bring to a boil then turn heat to low, simmer, and cook covered until tender. Remove about 1 quart of broth from pot and let cool down a little.

In a large bowl, beat eggs until frothy, slowly adding lemon juice. Slowly add the cooled broth to the egg mixture, a half ladle at a time, while still beating the egg mixture. After all the broth has been mixed in, slowly add to pot with the Dolmades.

Cover the pot and turn heat off. Let sit for about 10 minutes, then serve.

LOUISIANA BLUE CRAB

MOM WOULD BOIL CRABS, and out came the newspaper to cover the kitchen table. We'd gather around and sit, pick, and eat.

When I'm telling stories about growing up, I find myself saying, "We'd pick the meat for Mom and her dishes." But I know we were really picking for ourselves and hoping Mom would make crab bisque or stuffed crabs. The more we picked, the better the chances there would be for enough meat for all of her famous creations. And I never, ever minded the pickin' parties, as my folks would call them.

It was rare that we went to the store and bought live crabs. Every once in a while, maybe. Most of our crabs came from Dad and Uncle Chet sidelining them during their fishing outings. And that was most weekends.

Sometimes it was just me and Dad going fishing, and he would drive us out to Lake Pontchartrain.

Armed with tackle and fresh shrimp for bait, it was the plastic bag tightly rolled and sealed full of "ripe" chicken necks Mom had saved for Dad that was the lure for the crabs.

We'd make our way down the water, and Dad would tie a small rope to the crab net and on the other end would be a hook that he'd jam into a crevice in the seawall. He'd toss out that crab net perfectly baited with the two-week-old chicken neck. And we'd forget about it for a while to concentrate on our fishing. After about twenty minutes Dad would start checking for crabs. He'd carefully pull up the net, and it never failed that a couple of fat blue crabs would be latched on trying to get to that stinky bait. Dad would empty the crabs into a bushel basket lined with damp newspaper. He'd check the bait, and out the trap would go again. Before you knew it, the basket was as full as we dared.

Kevin's Take

Where flavor matters, claw meat has sweeter notes and adds the traditional flavors of crab to sauces and dishes. For my taste, I prefer using claw meat in my recipes.

Lump crabmeat comes from the body, which yields the large, prettier looking meat. When you want a visual pop or you are lightly handling the crabmeat, the lump meat is what you use. I decide which to use based on whether I'm counting on a strong flavor finish or a lighter note of crab flavor. Lump crabmeat is dramatic, where claw meat is the flavor intensifier and good for longer cooking times.

CRAB RAVIGOTE

Makes 12

---

4 cups lump crabmeat

1 cup Ravigote Sauce

12 frozen puff pastry shells, baked following the package directions

Combine crabmeat and Ravigote Sauce, and chill for 4-6 hours. Once chilled, fill pastry shells with Crab Ravigote and serve.

RAVIGOTE SAUCE

³/₄ cup mayonnaise

¹/₄ cup Creole mustard

2 tablespoons minced red bell pepper

2 tablespoons minced green onions

2 tablespoons lemon juice

1 tablespoon Worcestershire sauce

1 tablespoon minced anchovies

Stir together ingredients in a bowl and chill until ready to use.

CREOLE CRAB DIP

Serves 6

1 (8-ounce) package cream cheese, softened

½ cup mayonnaise

¼ cup grated Swiss cheese

¼ cup minced shallots

1 tablespoon fresh lemon juice

2 teaspoons hot sauce

2 teaspoons Worcestershire sauce

1 tablespoon Creole seasoning

1 teaspoon Creole mustard

1 tablespoon olive oil

2 tablespoons finely chopped red bell pepper

2 tablespoons finely chopped yellow bell pepper

1 tablespoon minced garlic

1 pound jumbo lump crabmeat

1 teaspoon kosher salt

½ teaspoon cayenne pepper

½ cup shredded Parmesan cheese

Green onion, sliced for garnish

Pita bread, or other toasted bread slices

Preheat oven to 350 degrees. Spray a 1-quart baking dish with nonstick cooking spray and set aside.

In a large bowl, combine cream cheese, mayonnaise, Swiss cheese, shallots, lemon juice, hot sauce, Worcestershire sauce, Creole seasoning, and Creole mustard. Beat at medium-high speed with a mixer until combined.

In a medium skillet, heat olive oil over medium-high heat. Add peppers and cook, stirring often, until tender, 2–3 minutes. Add garlic and crabmeat, and cook 1 minute.

Fold crabmeat mixture into cream cheese mixture. Season with salt and cayenne pepper. Transfer to a prepared baking dish. Sprinkle Parmesan on top of mixture.

Bake until mixture is hot and bubbly and cheese is light golden brown, about 25 minutes.

Remove from oven and let cool 10 minutes before serving. Garnish with green onion. Serve with pita bread that has been quartered, brushed with olive oil, and toasted in oven for 10 minutes.

CRAB CLAWS
WITH MARINARA SAUCE

Serves 4

---

8 tablespoons butter, divided

4 cloves garlic, minced

1 pound crab claws

1 tablespoon Creole Seasoning

1/2 teaspoon kosher salt

1 tablespoon lemon juice

1/4 cup dry white wine

1/4 cup sliced green onions

Parsley, for garnish

Melt 4 tablespoons of butter over medium heat. Add garlic and cooking for 1 minute. Add crab claws, Creole seasoning, and salt. Gently shake pan to evenly heat crab claws for 2 minutes. Add lemon juice, wine, and green onions. Shake the pan so it all mixes and cooks for another 2 minutes. Remove from heat and add remaining butter to melt. This will give the sauce a nice shine. Garnish with parsley to serve along with marinara to dip.

MARINARA SAUCE *Makes 3 cups*

2 tablespoons olive oil

2 large cloves garlic, minced

2 (28-ounce) cans peeled, crushed or diced tomatoes without salt

1 tablespoon chopped fresh oregano

2 tablespoons brown sugar

1 teaspoon kosher salt

1/4 teaspoon red pepper flakes

1 tablespoon Creole seasoning

1/2 cup roughly chopped fresh basil

Heat a large pot over medium-low heat. Once hot, add oil and garlic. Sauté briefly for 1 minute, stirring frequently, until barely golden brown. Then add tomatoes, oregano, brown sugar, salt, red pepper flakes, and Creole seasoning.

Bring to a simmer over medium heat. Then reduce heat to low and simmer, uncovered, for 30 minutes, stirring occasionally. Add basil and stir. Cook for 5 minutes more.

ÉTOUFFÉE

WHEN IT COMES TO FOOD here in New Orleans, we "dress" our po' boy sandwiches, which means adding lettuce, tomatoes, mayonnaise, and pickles. We use "earl" not oil, and we "étouffée" our beloved shellfish. Étouffée means "to smother" as in smothered pork chops or smothered chicken; it means cooked in a thick, flavorful sauce.

The love of sauce as a partner in classic dishes is our French culinary heritage colliding with Creole cooking traditions. Depending on where you are from, or who your momma and daddy might be, depends on if you étouffée or smother your food. Maybe it's as simple as someone thinking that it was easier to say "smother that chicken" instead of "étouffée that bird." Whatever the explanation, it's certainly a gift that étouffée made it out of the bayou and onto menus in the French Quarter.

Crawfish Étouffée became a widely known dish in the 1950s as it began to appear in cookbooks and on restaurant menus. It's heavily Cajun, and seems to be rooted in and around Breaux Bridge, Louisiana. Étouffée made with crawfish, and eventually shrimp, as the main ingredient fascinated those who had never been exposed to this style of cooking, while to other folks, it seemed quiet ordinary.

KEVIN'S TAKE

Toasting your flour allows you to use very little oil. This is key when creating lighter-style dishes, or when you need a toasted flavor to round out the dish. Perhaps you are familiar with a classic roux as the way to extract toasted flavors. You can achieve the same flavors by toasting flour on a baking sheet in the oven to make Dry Roux Flour (see page 111). I encourage you to make the effort to toast your flour and keep it on hand in the pantry. We are talking about a couple of hours of toasting, but it's pretty effortless. Once the flour is baked, you sift it and store it as you would your regular flour. Put it in the fridge, freezer, or an airtight container on the counter. Add this to your cooking routine today and you can cut the oil tomorrow.

MUSHROOM AND STEAK ÉTOUFFÉE
WITH CHEESY MASHED POTATO PATTIES

Serves 4 to 6

- 2 bone-in strip steaks
- 4 tablespoons vegetable oil, divided
- 4 tablespoons Creole seasoning, divided
- 1 cup diced onion
- 1 cup diced red onion
- ½ cup diced celery

- ½ cup diced green bell pepper
- 1 pound portobello mushrooms, sliced
- 3 tablespoons minced garlic
- ½ teaspoon black pepper
- 1½ teaspoons chopped thyme
- 1½ teaspoon chopped rosemary
- 1½ teaspoon chopped oregano

- ½ teaspoon kosher salt
- ½ cup Dry Roux Flour (page 111)
- 2 to 3 cups beef stock
- 2 tablespoons Worcestershire sauce
- ¼ cup chopped parsley
- ¼ cup sliced green onion

Pat steaks dry and coat with 1 tablespoon of oil then season with 2 tablespoons of Creole seasoning. Heat a large cast iron skillet over high heat and sear steaks for 3 minutes per side. Remove steaks to cutting board to rest.

Lower heat to medium then add remaining oil to skillet. Add onion, red onion, celery, and bell pepper and sauté for 2 minutes. Stir in mushrooms and garlic and cook for 2 minutes. Add pepper, thyme, rosemary, oregano, and salt; stir well. Sprinkle flour on vegetables, stir, then slowly add stock, ½ cup at a time, until you get a smooth gravy consistency. Simmer for 20 minutes, stirring often.

While étouffée simmers, cut steaks off the bones and cut the meat into 1-inch cubes. Add the bones to the skillet, cooking for 20 minutes, then add the steak, stir well, and cook for 5 minutes. Remove from heat, stir in parsley and green onions and serve over Cheesy Mashed Potato Patties (recipe follows).

continued

DRY ROUX FLOUR

8 cups all-purpose flour

Preheat oven to 375 degrees.

Divide flour onto 2 rimmed baking sheets, keeping flour 1 inch away from all sides.

Bake in oven for 3 hours, stirring every 30 minutes. Remove from oven, let cool, and sift. Store in an air-tight container.

CHEESY MASHED POTATO PATTIES *Makes 12 patties*

3 cups chilled mashed potatoes

2/3 cup grated cheddar cheese

2 tablespoons chopped
  green onions

1 egg, lightly beaten

1/2 teaspoon kosher salt, plus extra

3 tablespoons all-purpose flour

1/2 cup all-purpose flour

2 tablespoons Creole seasoning

Vegetable oil, for pan-frying

In a large bowl, stir together the mashed potatoes, cheese, green onions, egg, salt, and 3 tablespoons flour until combined. Divide the mixture into 12 portions. Roll each portion into a compact ball then flatten it into a patty about a 1/2 inch thick.

Place 1/2 cup flour in a shallow dish and stir in Creole seasoning. Carefully dredge each patty in the flour.

Heat enough vegetable oil to thoroughly coat the bottom of a large sauté pan over medium heat.

Fry the pancakes, in batches, until they're golden brown and crispy on both sides, 3-4 minutes. Add more oil to the pan as needed between batches. Transfer the pancakes to a paper towel-lined plate and immediately sprinkle them with salt.

PORK AND ONION ÉTOUFFÉE

Serves 4 to 6

6 bone-in pork chops

3 tablespoons Creole seasoning, divided

3 tablespoons oil

2 onions, halved and sliced

½ cup diced celery

½ cup diced green bell pepper

½ teaspoon ground cumin

½ teaspoon cayenne pepper

1 teaspoon thyme

1 teaspoon kosher salt

2 tablespoons minced garlic

½ cup Dry Roux Flour (page 111)

2 to 3 cups ham stock

2 bay leaves

¼ cup parsley

¼ cup sliced green onions

Rice, to serve

Rinse and pat pork chops dry. Season with 2 tablespoons of Creole seasoning and set aside.

In a deep skillet, heat oil over medium heat, add onions, celery, and bell pepper and sauté for 5 minutes. Add remaining Creole seasoning, cumin, cayenne, thyme, and salt and stir well; add garlic. After 1 minute, sprinkle in the flour, stir, and start adding stock, ½ cup at a time, until reaching a thick gravy texture.

Add bay leaves and pork chops. Cover, and simmer for 20–30 minutes depending on the thickness of the pork chops, stirring occasionally. Remove from heat and add parsley and green onions and serve over rice.

GULF FISH ÉTOUFFÉE

Serves 4 to 6

3 (8-ounce) drum fillets or any white, firm, and flaky fish, cut into thirds

3 tablespoons Creole seasoning, divided

4 tablespoons butter

1 cup diced onion

½ cup diced celery

½ cup diced red bell pepper

1 clove garlic, minced

½ teaspoon white pepper

1 teaspoon kosher salt

2 tablespoons lemon zest

½ cup Dry Roux Flour (page 111)

2 to 3 cups seafood stock

2 tablespoons lemon juice

1 tablespoon Worcestershire sauce

1 teaspoon hot sauce

¼ cup chopped parsley

½ cup sliced green onions

Rice, for serving

Rinse, pat fish dry, and season with 2 tablespoons of Creole seasoning. Place in refrigerator to chill.

Melt butter in large skillet over medium heat. Add onion, celery, and bell pepper and sauté for 5 minutes. Add garlic, pepper, salt, and lemon zest, stirring for 2 minutes. Sprinkle in flour, stir, and slowly add stock, ½ cup at a time, until you get the consistency of gravy.

Stir in lemon juice, Worcestershire sauce, and hot sauce; reduce heat and simmer for 10 minutes. Stir well and gently place fish in sauce and cook, covered, for 10 minutes. Remove cover and add parsley and green onions.

Place rice on serving dish, and using a spoon, gently lay fish over rice, add sauce, and serve.

BASTILLE DAY

GRANDMA EMILY, MY DAD'S MOM, spoke a language with her aunt that, as a child, I just thought was how adults spoke. I figured that once I grew up I'd start speaking like that, too. Well as it turned out, they were speaking fluent French. And that's not unusual for our local families in Louisiana. Most native New Orleanians have a little seasoning in their DNA that is French, Native American, Spanish, or African.

When I was in elementary school and learning New Orleans history, I found out about our customs and traditions from the Native Americans. The French culture remained strong, and was flavored and seasoned with the African influences and Spanish heritage that has come to universally be known as Creole. Creole is hard to define, specifically because it literally means the first born in a new colony of foreign parents.

So whatever mix or percentage of immigrant nationality, you can be any version of Creole in New Orleans. I am very proud to identify as a Creole New Orleanian.

I stay connected to my French side by attending the Bastille Day festivities in the French Quarter every year. Around July 14, which is thought of as French Independence Day or French National Day, New Orleanians call to mind and honor our French roots by celebrating in the heart of the French Quarter. It's clear that back in 1789, although under Spanish rule, New Orleans was filled with citizens who identified as French and were waiting to hear news of the uprising.

Celebrating the past helps keep it in the present. New Orleanians have a voracious appetite for celebration, and Bastille Day is one of those real connections that keeps our roots alive.

KEVIN'S TAKE
Teaching kids our history is one of the most valuable gifts we can give to our family. I've made an effort to show Kevin, Jonathan, and Noah my culture. I want to show my sons New Orleans and Louisiana culture as it pertains to my family background.

I do that with food. Most every family has a signature dish or two. Write them down and pass them around. It's a small effort that is filled with joy. And it's as easy as jotting down a quick recipe and gifting it to someone important to you. It will open up conversations with family that leads to laughter, sharing memories, and keeping your family connected. Give it a try.

CHICKEN LIVER PÂTÉ

Makes 4 cups

1 pound chicken livers, well-trimmed

1 onion, thinly sliced

2 cloves garlic, minced

2 bay leaves

$^{1}/_{2}$ teaspoon thyme leaves

1 teaspoon kosher salt

1 cup water

$^{1}/_{2}$ cup butter, room temperature

$1^{1}/_{2}$ tablespoons cognac

Salt and freshly ground pepper, to taste

Toasted baguette slices, for serving

In a medium saucepan, combine the chicken livers, onion, garlic, bay leaves, thyme, and salt. Add the water and bring to a simmer. Cover, reduce heat to low, and cook, stirring occasionally, until the livers are barely pink inside, about 3 minutes. Remove from the heat and let stand, covered, for 5 minutes.

Discard the bay leaves. Using a slotted spoon, transfer the livers, onion, and garlic to a food processor; process until coarsely puréed. With the machine on, add the butter, 2 tablespoons at a time, until incorporated. Add the cognac, season with salt and pepper, and process until completely smooth. Scrape the pâté into 4 or 5 large ramekins. Press a piece of plastic wrap directly onto the surface of the pâté and refrigerate for 4–6 hours or until firm. Serve cold with sliced and toasted baguette.

CRUSTLESS SPINACH AND LEEK QUICHE

Serves 6 to 8

---

1 tablespoon vegetable oil

1 cup chopped onion

1 cup sliced fresh mushrooms

1 cup thinly sliced leeks

1 tablespoon Creole seasoning

$\frac{1}{2}$ teaspoon kosher salt

1 bunch spinach, chopped

$\frac{2}{3}$ cup finely chopped
cooked ham

5 large eggs

3 cups grated Monterey
Jack cheese

$\frac{1}{8}$ teaspoon pepper

Preheat oven to 350 degrees.

In a large skillet, heat oil and sauté onion, mushrooms, and leeks until tender. Add Creole seasoning, salt, spinach, and ham; cook and stir until the excess moisture has evaporated. Cool slightly. Beat eggs in a large bowl then add cheese and mix well. Stir in spinach mixture and pepper; blend well. Spread evenly into a greased 9 x 9-inch baking dish. Bake for 30–35 minutes or until a knife inserted in center comes out clean.

STONE FRUIT GALETTE

Serves 8

DOUGH

1½ cups all-purpose flour

¼ cup finely ground
white cornmeal

1 tablespoon sugar

¼ teaspoon kosher salt

½ cup cold unsalted butter, cubed

¼ cup ice water, divided

FRUIT FILLING

1 to 1½ pounds stone fruit
(plums, nectarines, or peaches),
halved, pitted, and cut into
¼- to ½-inch-thick slices

¼ cup raw sugar, plus
more for sprinkling

1 tablespoon all-purpose flour

1 teaspoon ground cinnamon

½ teaspoon freshly
grated nutmeg

¼ teaspoon kosher salt

1 tablespoon unsalted
butter, cubed

1 large egg

1 tablespoon plus 1 teaspoon
water, divided

1 tablespoon light-colored jam
(such as peach, apple, or pear)

DOUGH Pulse the flour, cornmeal, sugar, and salt together in a food processor. Add the butter and pulse until the mixture looks like coarse crumbs, about 10 pulses. It's okay if there are a few larger pieces of butter. Drizzle in 2 tablespoons of the water and pulse until dough is crumbly in texture but holds together when squeezed, about 4 pulses. If the mixture is dry, pulse in up to 2 more tablespoons water, 1 tablespoon at a time.

Turn the dough out onto a piece of plastic wrap. Flatten into a disk and wrap completely in the plastic wrap. Refrigerate for 30 minutes.

Preheat oven to 400 degrees.

Unwrap the dough and place it on a piece of parchment paper. Cover with a second piece of parchment. Roll the dough into a 12-inch round about ⅛ inch thick. Slide the parchment and the dough onto a baking sheet and remove the top layer of parchment.

FRUIT FILLING Place fruit, ¼ cup sugar, flour, cinnamon, nutmeg, and salt in a large bowl and gently combine.

Pile the fruit mixture onto the dough, slightly mounding it in the center, and leaving a 2-inch border around the edge. Fold the rim of the dough up and over the edge of the filling, overlapping and pleating the dough as you go.

continued

Evenly distribute the cubes of butter across the top of the fruit.

Beat the egg with 1 tablespoon water. Brush the crust with the egg wash and sprinkle with sugar.

Bake until the crust is a deep golden brown and the fruit is cooked, 30–35 minutes. Transfer the parchment with the galette on it to a wire rack and cool completely.

Dilute jam with 1 teaspoon of water. Brush the fruit with the glaze. Cut the galette into wedges and serve.

Note: Dough can be made up to 3 days in advance and stored in the refrigerator, or frozen for up to 3 months.

FRIED CHICKEN

DO YOU REMEMBER those Magnalite roasting sets? Mom had the really big, deep skillet. When I saw Mom pull that out, I knew we were having fried chicken. I cherished that pan. I lost it in Hurricane Katrina, but I did not lose the memories or Mom's technique for making the perfect New Orleans fried chicken. I still have that.

Mom's fried chicken was legendary. And when family gathered at our house for the Fourth of July, or to watch the Saints game on television, she kept us well-fed. Mom had mastered the art of frying up triple batches of legs, thighs, breasts, and wings and holding them in the oven at the perfect temperature. That is an art in and of itself. It didn't matter if Mom's chicken was freshly fried or held in the oven for an hour as there was no difference in taste or texture. With Mom's culinary talent, we rarely ordered fried chicken out. There was no comparison—except, maybe, at Chez Helene.

Chez Helene was the brainchild of one of my mentors, Chef Austin Leslie. As a kid, we'd go eat there, and I discovered his fried chicken was almost as good as Mom's. Visitors from all over the world came to eat Chef Austin's cuisine, and to enjoy New Orleans-style fried chicken. Crescent City fried chicken is a perfect balance of salty, spicy, and crispy.

Kevin's Take

Pan fry, not deep fry. It's all about the turn when it comes to pan frying chicken. Pan frying chicken is what most of us are going to do at home. And I think any skillet you have, and like to use, is perfectly good. It just needs to be deep—about 3 inches deep.

I start with at least 1½ inches of oil and heat it up on high heat. Start by placing the larger pieces—the breasts in the middle of the pan, then put the thighs in next. The legs and wings go around the edge. By the time you've battered and placed all the pieces in the skillet, it is time to turn the breasts.

Basically, you want to have turned everything in the pan every minute to a minute and half. And, keep turning. The color will be even, and most importantly, the chicken will cook evenly. This was fried chicken advice from the best—Chef Austin Leslie.

SWEET HEAT PAN-FRIED CHICKEN

Serves 4 to 6

---

2 (3½–4-pound) chickens, each cut into 10 pieces (breasts halved)

6 tablespoons Creole seasoning, divided

1 tablespoon freshly ground black pepper

2 tablespoons plus 4 teaspoons kosher salt

4 large eggs

2 cups buttermilk

2 tablespoons hot sauce

4 cups all-purpose flour

Vegetable oil, for frying (about 10 cups)

2 tablespoons cayenne pepper

2 tablespoons dark brown sugar

1 teaspoon chili powder

1 teaspoon garlic powder

1 teaspoon paprika

Sliced pickles

Toss chicken with 4 tablespoons Creole seasoning, black pepper, and 2 tablespoons salt in a large bowl. Cover and chill at least 3 hours.

Whisk eggs, buttermilk, and hot sauce in a large bowl. Whisk flour and remaining salt in another large bowl.

Fit a Dutch oven with a thermometer; pour in oil to measure 2 inches. Heat over medium-high heat until thermometer registers 325 degrees.

Pat chicken dry. Working with 1 piece at a time, dredge in flour mixture, shaking off excess, then dip in buttermilk mixture, letting excess drip back into bowl. Dredge again in flour mixture and place on a baking sheet.

Working in 4 batches, and returning oil to 325 degrees between batches, fry chicken, turning occasionally, until skin is deep golden brown and crisp and an instant-read thermometer inserted into thickest part of pieces registers 160 degrees for white meat and 165 degrees for dark, 15–18 minutes. Transfer to a clean wire rack set inside a baking sheet. Let oil cool slightly.

Whisk remaining Creole seasoning, cayenne, brown sugar, chili powder, garlic powder, and paprika in a medium bowl; carefully whisk in 1 cup frying oil. Brush fried chicken with spicy oil. Serve with pickles.

CHICKEN SALAD SLIDERS

Serves 6

3/4 cup mayonnaise

1/4 cup buttermilk

1/4 cup Creole mustard

1 1/2 teaspoons Italian seasoning

1 tablespoon Creole seasoning

1/2 teaspoon celery salt

1 tablespoon fresh lemon juice

4 cups diced leftover cold fried chicken

1/4 cup chopped fresh parsley

1/4 cup finely diced celery

1/2 cup thinly sliced green onions

Kosher salt and freshly ground black pepper, to taste

12 slider buns

Whisk together the mayonnaise, buttermilk, mustard, Italian seasoning, Creole seasoning, celery salt, and lemon juice in a large bowl.

Add in the chicken, parsley, celery, and green onions. Stir gently to combine. Add salt and pepper. Cover and refrigerate for 30 minutes before serving on slider buns.

CHICKEN AND WAFFLE MELT

Serves 8

MARINADE

8 boneless, skinless chicken thighs

1 cup buttermilk

2 tablespoons hot sauce

2 tablespoons Creole seasoning

½ teaspoon kosher salt

½ teaspoon pepper

1 teaspoon smoked paprika

⅛ teaspoon cayenne pepper

½ teaspoon kosher salt

1 teaspoon Creole seasoning

1 teaspoon garlic powder

1 cup buttermilk

Vegetable oil, for frying

TO FRY

1¼ cups all-purpose flour

½ cup cornmeal

WAFFLES

1 cup all-purpose flour

1 cup yellow cornmeal

2 teaspoons double-acting baking powder

½ teaspoon baking soda

¼ teaspoon kosher salt

2 cups buttermilk

2 eggs

4 tablespoons butter, melted

¼ cup cane syrup, plus extra

1 cup grated cheddar cheese, plus extra

1 bunch green onions, sliced

CHICKEN Place a large piece of plastic wrap on the counter. Place 1 chicken thigh at a time in the center of the plastic wrap and fold half the plastic over the top of the chicken. Use the flat side of a meat mallet to pound the chicken to an even ½-inch thickness. Set aside.

Pour the buttermilk and hot sauce into a ziplock bag; seal and massage the ingredients together. Season the chicken thighs with Creole seasoning, salt, and pepper and add them to the marinade. Seal the bag. Let the chicken marinate in the refrigerator for at least 4 hours or overnight and then discard marinade.

TO FRY Preheat oven to 250 degrees.

Set up 2 shallow bowls for dredging. In 1 bowl, whisk together the flour, cornmeal, paprika, cayenne, salt, Creole seasoning, and garlic powder. Add the buttermilk to the other bowl.

In a medium heavy-bottom skillet or Dutch oven, heat about 1 inch oil over medium to medium-high heat until it's between 350 and 375 degrees.

Working in batches, dip chicken into flour mixture, then into the buttermilk, and into the flour mixture a second time. Tap off excess

continued

flour and gently place chicken into the hot oil. Do not crowd the pan. Fry for 6–8 minutes, turning occasionally with tongs until the chicken is crispy and a deep golden brown. Transfer cooked chicken to a baking sheet lined with paper towels to drain. Place the baking sheet in the oven to keep chicken warm.

WAFFLES In a large bowl, combine flour, cornmeal, baking powder, baking soda, and salt. Whisk together and set aside.

In a smaller bowl, combine buttermilk, eggs, butter, and cane syrup; whisk thoroughly. Add wet ingredients to dry ingredients and stir until just mixed. Stir in the cheese and green onions.

Preheat waffle iron. Lightly coat with vegetable spray if necessary. Scoop batter onto the center of the waffle iron. Close the lid and bake until browned and crisp, 5–7 minutes. Place waffles on a baking sheet and keep warm in the oven while you continue cooking the rest of the batter.

To serve, place chicken on plate and top with a waffle. Drizzle with additional syrup and a sprinkle of cheese, if desired. Top with another piece of chicken and serve.

OKTOBERFEST

GERMAN IMMIGRANTS TO NEW ORLEANS are credited for introducing the accordion to the Cajuns. And the same can be said for the establishment of farms on the outskirts of New Orleans, in particular, an area named Lac des Allemande, The German Coast. Germans also founded several bakeries, including Binder's and Leidenheimer's, both of which have been in business for over 100 years. It was the German immigrants who first baked and delivered the baguettes throughout the city.

Kolb's was the first German restaurant I ever went to. It was a mainstay in New Orleans from 1899 until it closed in 1994. My entire family would meet there to dine on German specialties, particularly schnitzel and sauerkraut. I really didn't put two and two together until I began traveling Louisiana leading tour groups, but Mom's paneed meat was basically schnitzel. Creole to German. I think it's pretty interesting.

To panee meat, or coat in breadcrumbs, is a French technique. It's a great way to take a lower-grade cut of meat and turn it into a delicious dish. So panee is a verb. It's what you do to the meat. And the Germans do the same. It's called schnitzel, but schnitzel is a noun, the name of the dish.

German culture is deeply rooted in New Orleans, and there is no better place to enjoy it than at the annual Oktoberfest celebration hosted by Deutsches Haus. Focused on German food, the descendants of the early German settlers offer music, dance, and traditional dress as a way to honor and keep German influences alive.

I've attended Oktoberfest many times over the years, but in 2017, I had the opportunity to hang out behind the scenes with the cooks. It's impressive to see volunteers turn into professionals turning out authentic recipes from their outdoor kitchen. Guys grilling sausages, teams in the pot cooking area monitoring the sauerkraut production, brats, German pretzels, German-style potato salad, schnitzel, and red cabbage; it's all there and all being done the traditional way.

Kevin's Take

Panee is a great technique to master and it's quite simple. Ask your butcher to direct you to meat called cutlets. And mention what you are cooking. The butcher will know exactly what you need. To prepare, place the cutlets between two sheets of unwaxed parchment paper and pound them out super thin. Then bread and fry in about $1/2$ inch of oil. They fry very quickly. With the seasoned breadcrumbs and properly seasoned cutlets, you have mastered both the French panee and German schnitzel.

GERMAN SAUSAGE
WITH CAJUN POUTINE

Serves 8

FRIES

3 large russet potatoes, scrubbed

Ice water in a large bowl

Vegetable oil, for frying

Salt, to taste

GRAVY

8 tablespoons butter

½ cup all-purpose flour

¼ cup diced onion

1 tablespoon Creole seasoning

1 tablespoon minced garlic

2 to 3 cups beef stock

1 teaspoon Worcestershire sauce

¼ cup chopped parsley

¼ cup sliced green onion

TO SERVE

1½ cups cheddar cheese curds or torn chunks of mozzarella

8 pan-fried or grilled bratwurst links

FRIES Cut potatoes into uniform pieces, about ¼ inch thick and 4 inches long. As you cut, drop the potatoes into the ice water and leave them there until you are ready to fry them. Drain and pat dry.

In a deep skillet, bring your oil up to 375 degrees. Fry potatoes in small batches for about 2 minutes per batch. Remove and drain.

Once all potatoes have had the first fry, fry potatoes again for about 3 minutes at 375 degrees or until they start to turn golden brown. Be sure to fry in small batches and allow the temperature of the oil to come back to 375 degrees after each fry. Drain on paper towels and lightly salt.

GRAVY In a skillet, melt butter over medium heat and add flour. Cook, stirring constantly until flour turns a deep peanut butter color, 6–8 minutes. Stir in onion, Creole seasoning, and garlic, then slowly add beef stock until you have a gravy consistency. Add Worcestershire sauce, parsley, and green onions. Stir to blend.

TO SERVE Place fried potatoes on serving plates, cover with gravy, and top with cheese curds. Serve sausage alongside.

PORK SCHNITZEL
WITH BACON-APPLE SAUERKRAUT

Serves 4 to 6

---

2 pounds boneless pork chops, trimmed and sliced into 1/2-inch-thick cutlets

1/2 cup all-purpose flour

1 tablespoon garlic powder

1/2 teaspoon paprika

1/2 teaspoon freshly ground black pepper

1 tablespoon Creole seasoning

1/2 teaspoon kosher salt

3 large eggs, beaten

2 cups breadcrumbs

Vegetable oil, for frying

Lemon wedges

Line a cutting board with plastic wrap, place cutlets in a single layer on cutting board, and cover with plastic wrap. Pound cutlets with a meat mallet or the back of a heavy saucepan, until 1/4 inch to 1/8 inch thick.

Set up 3 bowls. In the first, combine the flour, garlic powder, paprika, pepper, Creole seasoning, and salt. Place the eggs in the second bowl, and the breadcrumbs in the third bowl.

Dredge both sides of each pounded cutlet in the flour then dip in the egg, letting excess egg drip back into the bowl, before dredging in breadcrumbs.

Once all cutlets are breaded, heat a large pan over medium heat and add enough oil to cover the bottom of the pan. When oil is hot, add breaded cutlets, a few at a time, and sauté 2–3 minutes on each side or until cooked through. Remove to a paper towel-lined plate. Serve with lemon wedges and Bacon-Apple Sauerkraut.

BACON-APPLE SAUERKRAUT *Serves 6 to 8*

6 tablespoons butter

4 slices bacon, cut into 1/2-inch pieces

2 cups thinly sliced onions

3 tart apples, thinly sliced

2 pounds sauerkraut, drained and rinsed

12 ounces beer, of choice

1/2 teaspoon kosher salt

1 teaspoon pepper

1/2 teaspoon caraway seeds

Melt butter in a large heavy pot over medium-high heat. Add bacon and cook, stirring often, until fat has started to render, about 5 minutes.

Toss onion and apples in the fat and cook, stirring occasionally, until onions begin to soften, about 3 minutes. Stir in sauerkraut.

Add beer and season with salt, pepper, and caraway seeds. Bring mixture to a boil and cover. Reduce heat to just simmering and cook for 45 minutes. Stir and serve hot.

LAUGENBREZEL
(TRADITIONAL GERMAN PRETZELS) WITH BEER-CHEESE SAUCE

Makes 2 large or 4 small pretzels

1½ tablespoons barley malt syrup or ½ tablespoon molasses

1 (¼-ounce) package active dry yeast

1½ cups warm water

3 tablespoons unsalted butter, softened, plus more for serving

4 cups all-purpose flour, plus more for dusting

¼ teaspoon kosher salt

2 tablespoons baking soda

1 cup water

Coarse salt, for sprinkling

Preheat a baking stone in oven to 500 degrees.

Stir together syrup, yeast, and warm water in a large bowl and let set until foamy, about 10 minutes. Add butter, flour, and ¼ teaspoon salt and stir until dough forms. Transfer to a lightly floured work surface and knead until smooth and elastic, about 8 minutes.

Cut dough in half, and working with one half at a time, roll dough into a 4-foot rope, about 1 inch thick. Transfer rope to the bottom edge of a sheet of parchment paper, and keeping the center of the rope on the paper, pick up both ends, cross one end over the other, about 2 inches from the ends, and twist; attach each end to the sides of the pretzel. Repeat with remaining dough and set aside to rest for 20 minutes.

Bring baking soda and 1 cup water to a simmer in a 2-quart saucepan over medium-high heat, stirring constantly until baking soda dissolves. Brush each pretzel generously with the baking soda solution, sprinkle with coarse salt, and using a sharp paring knife, make a 6-inch slash, about ¼-inch deep across the bottom edge of the pretzel.

Working one at a time, slide pretzel on parchment paper onto the hot stone and bake until dark brown, about 15 minutes. Repeat with remaining pretzel. Let cool for about 10 minutes. Serve warm with Beer Cheese Sauce.

continued

BEER-CHEESE SAUCE *Makes 3 cups*

2 tablespoons butter

1/2 cup finely chopped onion

2 tablespoons all-purpose flour

1 cup beer, of choice

3/4 cup heavy cream

1 teaspoon garlic powder

1 teaspoon Creole Seasoning

1/2 cup grated sharp
  cheddar cheese

1/2 cup grated Swiss cheese

Melt butter in a saucepan over medium heat. Add onion, cooking for 2 minutes. Add flour and cook, stirring constantly, for 2 minutes. Whisk in beer until smooth. Reduce heat and cook for 4 minutes. Add cream and garlic powder, stirring until thick, about 5 minutes. Remove from heat, add Creole seasoning and whisk in cheeses until completely melted. Keep warm to serve.

THE POWDERY BEIGNET

MOST PEOPLE CELEBRATE a visit to New Orleans by eating a beignet. They head to the French Quarter and line up at Café du Monde. Or after a visit to New Orleans' City Park, they saunter over to the old casino building and enjoy Morning Call's version. These piping hot, sweet fried fritters are the French version of a donut, without the hole. It's on everyone's to-do list when visiting New Orleans.

As a kid, I remember asking if we could get coffee and donuts. How much time we had determined where we went. There are two iconic beignet cafés in New Orleans. Café du Monde in the French Quarter and Morning Call out in City Park.

The original Morning Call at the French Market had car service. They'd bring your beignets right to the car. Oh man, I loved that. Bags of beignets dusted with sugar. It was a little hard to eat them in the car while driving on our streets in New Orleans. My mom would say, "Wait 'til you get home." I'd try to sneak a bite and we would hit a bump. The beignet would hit me in the forehead and powdered sugar would go everywhere.

If we had more time, or friends visiting us, Dad would park the car and we would sit down at Café du Monde, a magical setting with the hustle and bustle of passersby. Sharp-dressed servers carried trays of beignets piled high and dusted with powdered sugar piled even higher. That was one of the great times of being an only child. I got my own plate of beignets and didn't have to share.

KEVIN'S TAKE The secret to making a quick beignet? Grab a can of biscuit dough, roll the biscuits out, toss them in oil to deep fry, and poof—golden brown and with dusting of powdered sugar. It's like you're right there on the banks of the Mississippi River in the heart of the French Quarter. That's what my Mom did if we didn't have time to run downtown.

BEIGNETS
WITH CHOCOLATE SAUCE

Serves 8 to 10

---

1 cup warm water

³/₄ cup sugar, divided

1 (¹/₄-ounce) package
active dry yeast

2 large eggs, beaten

1¹/₄ teaspoons kosher salt

1 cup evaporated milk

6¹/₂ cups all-purpose flour, divided

¹/₄ cup shortening

Vegetable oil, for frying

2 cups powdered sugar

In the bowl of a stand mixer, or in a large bowl, combine water, ¹/₄ cup sugar, and yeast and let set for 10 minutes.

In a separate bowl, whisk the eggs, salt, milk, and remaining sugar together. Add the egg mixture to the yeast starter and stir. Add 3 cups of flour and combine thoroughly. Cut in the shortening and continue to mix. Add remaining flour and mix to form a large dough ball.

On a floured work surface, knead the dough until smooth, about 10 minutes. Place dough into a large bowl, cover, and place in a warm place to rise, about 2 hours.

Preheat oil to 375 degrees.

Roll out the dough to a ¹/₄-inch-thick rectangle and cut into 2-inch squares. Fry pieces to a golden brown, turning continuously. Remove and drain on paper towels. Sprinkle with powdered sugar and drizzle with Chocolate Sauce, or serve sauce on the side for dipping.

CHOCOLATE SAUCE *Makes 2 cups*

¹/₃ cup sugar

1 cup milk

2 cups semisweet chocolate chips

1 teaspoon vanilla

¹/₄ teaspoon kosher salt

In a saucepan, stir together sugar and milk and bring to a simmer. Add chocolate chips, remove from heat, and stir until chocolate is melted and incorporated. Add vanilla and salt and stir until smooth. Serve warm or cold.

LOBSTER BEIGNETS

Serves 6

3 tablespoons butter

½ cup finely chopped sweet onion

¼ cup finely chopped
   red bell pepper

2 cloves garlic, minced

1 tablespoon Creole seasoning

½ teaspoon kosher salt

2 cups chopped lobster meat

½ cup sliced green onions

¼ cup chopped parsley

1 tablespoon tomato paste

4 ounces cream cheese

½ cup grated Parmesan cheese

Vegetable oil, for frying

1 recipe Beignet dough (page
   "Beignets" on page 140)

In a large skillet over medium heat, melt butter and sauté onion and bell pepper, about 3 minutes. Add garlic, Creole seasoning, and salt, cooking for 1 minute. Add lobster, green onions, and parsley, cooking for about 4 minutes until heated. Add tomato paste and incorporate, then add cream cheese and Parmesan cheese. Remove from heat and stir until cheese is melted. Pour into a bowl to cool for 10 minutes.

Preheat oil to 375 degrees.

Place dough onto a floured surface and roll out to a ¼- to ⅛-inch thickness. Cut dough into 3-inch pieces. Place a teaspoon of lobster filling in the center of half of the dough pieces. Moisten the edges of the dough with water and top with another piece of dough. Using a fork, press edges to seal. Gently place in oil and fry to a golden brown, turning often. Remove and drain on paper towels before serving.

HERBED HAM AND CHEESE BEIGNETS

Serves 6

Vegetable oil, for frying

½ pound sliced ham

½ pound sliced Swiss cheese

1 recipe Beignet dough
(page"Beignets" on page 140)

¼ cup Creole mustard

1 cup chopped basil leaves

Preheat oil to 375 degrees.

Cut ham and cheese into 2-inch pieces.

Place dough onto a floured surface and roll out to a ¼- to ⅛-inch thickness. Cut dough into 3-inch pieces. Spread half the dough pieces with mustard, then top with ham, cheese, and a pinch of basil. Moisten edge of dough with water and top with another piece of dough. Using a fork, press edges to seal. Gently place in oil and fry until golden brown, turning often. Remove and drain on paper towels before serving.

NEW ORLEANS NEIGHBORHOODS

THE FRERET AREA IN UPTOWN New Orleans is hopping. It's one of those New Orleans neighborhoods that have enjoyed a resurgence. Back when I was growing up on Valance Street, whatever we needed, we could walk a few blocks to Freret Street and purchase. It was our neighborhood Main Street.

As time passes, as with all neighborhoods, the rhythm of life ebbs and flows. Change is the glorious part of New Orleans neighborhoods. After Hurricane Katrina, neighborhoods came back bigger and stronger than ever before. Each neighborhood, having a different character and personality, has worked to bring back shopping, dining, architecture, and of course, their signature festival.

A shining example of this are the wildly successful Oat Street Po' Boy Festival and the Freret Street Festival. They are two of the finest examples of neighborhoods getting together to celebrate the unique charm of their streets, people, and food.

My favorite thing about these festivals is the interaction with the community. Watching the kids play with each other and the younger families interacting with the older families is very joyful. That's community and there is no better place to do that than out in the streets of New Orleans.

The recipes in this chapter are tasty examples of what you can find at many neighborhood festivals—good local eats.

KEVIN'S TAKE I'm fascinated by funnel cakes. I love to watch them being made. They are super easy to make, smell so good, and that powdered sugar is so New Orleans. Funnel cakes make people happy, and they are a part of neighborhood celebrations.

CHEESESTEAK PO' BOY

Serves 4

---

1 (24-ounce) rib-eye steak

4 tablespoons vegetable oil, divided

2 cups thinly sliced onions

2 tablespoons minced garlic

2 tablespoons Creole seasoning

1/2 teaspoon kosher salt

1/2 teaspoon black pepper

Mayonnaise, to taste

Creole mustard, to taste

1 po' boy loaf

6 slices provolone cheese

Place beef in freezer for 2–3 hours then thinly slice.

In a cast iron skillet over medium heat, add 2 tablespoons oil and onions. Cook for about 3 minutes to allow onions to soften but not brown. Stir in garlic and remove mixture from pan.

Increase the heat, add remaining oil to the pan, and when pan is hot, add beef, Creole seasoning, salt, and pepper. Quickly sear the meat until browned, but do not dry it out. Stir in onion mixture and mix well. Remove from heat.

Spread mayonnaise and/or Creole mustard on bottom of bread. Add meat and onions and then top with cheese. Place the top of the bread on the sandwich and slice into 4 pieces.

RED VELVET FUNNEL CAKES
WITH CREAM CHEESE DRIZZLE

Serves 6

3 to 4 cups vegetable
  oil, for frying

2 cups all-purpose flour

1 tablespoon cocoa powder

1/2 teaspoon baking powder

1/2 teaspoon kosher salt

1/4 cup sugar

1 teaspoon light brown sugar

1 1/2 cups milk

1 teaspoon pure vanilla extract

2 eggs

1 tablespoon apple cider vinegar

1/2 teaspoon baking soda

2 tablespoons red food coloring

1/3 cup powdered sugar,
  for dusting

Heat oil, 2 inches deep, in a medium skillet over medium-high heat.

Whisk flour, cocoa powder, baking powder, salt, sugar, brown sugar, milk, vanilla, eggs, vinegar, baking soda, and red food coloring together in a large bowl.

Pour 1/2 cup of batter into a ziplock bag or plastic squeeze bottle with a spout. Snip a small bit of the corner of the bag off, or you may have to cut the spout on the squeeze bottle to make spout a little wider. The squeeze bottle is easier to use.

Squeeze the batter in a circular motion into the oil. Let it cook for about 1 minute before flipping to the other side to cook for another minute. Remove to a plate lined with paper towels to drain. Sprinkle with a generous amount of powdered sugar and then top with Cream Cheese Drizzle and serve warm.

CREAM CHEESE DRIZZLE *Makes 2 cups*

8 ounces cream cheese, softened

1 cup sour cream

1/2 cup sugar

1 teaspoon vanilla

1 to 2 tablespoons lemon juice

Mix all ingredients until well-blended. Serve immediately, or cover and refrigerate until ready to use.

PARMESAN-GARLIC CHICKEN WINGS
AND GREENS

Serves 6

---

1 teaspoon dried oregano

1 teaspoon dried rosemary

1/2 teaspoon ground cumin

1/2 teaspoon white pepper

1 teaspoon kosher salt

2 1/2 pounds chicken wings

3 tablespoons butter, melted

2 tablespoons minced fresh basil

2 cloves garlic, finely minced

1/4 cup grated Parmesan cheese

1 teaspoon Creole seasoning

Preheat oven to 425 degrees.

In a small bowl, mix together the oregano, rosemary, cumin, pepper, and salt. Place chicken wings in a bowl and season with this mixture.

Line a baking sheet with aluminum foil and spray a cooling rack with oil. Set the rack on the baking sheet and place the chicken wings on the rack. Cooking the wings on the rack will crisp them on all sides. Bake the chicken wings for 20-25 minutes.

While the chicken is baking, mix together the butter, basil, garlic, cheese, and Creole seasoning. When the chicken is cooked through, toss the wings with the butter sauce. Serve the wings with a side of Greens.

continued

GREENS *Serves 8*

1 pound collard greens, cleaned and cut

1 pound mustard greens, cleaned and cut

1 pound turnip greens, cleaned and cut

1 pound bacon, chopped

2 cups diced onions

1 tablespoon minced garlic

8 cups chicken broth

1 tablespoon Creole seasoning

1/2 teaspoon ground black pepper

2 to 3 tablespoons white distilled vinegar

1/2 teaspoon kosher salt

2 tablespoons sugar

Thoroughly wash greens to remove any grit and chop into small pieces.

Place the bacon in a pot over medium heat. Brown the bacon and then add in the onions. Cook until the onions start to sweat. Add in the garlic; cook for 1 minute. Pour in the broth and turn the heat up to high, bringing to a boil.

Add the greens into the pot in batches. Once all of the greens are in the pot, sprinkle in the Creole seasoning and pepper. Add the vinegar, salt, and sugar and stir. Cover the pot and let simmer for 1 hour over medium heat. Be sure to stir periodically.

SHRIMP

LOUISIANA HAS OVER 7000 MILES of shoreline, which includes not only the Gulf of Mexico shores but our lakes, rivers, and estuary marshes. Louisiana is called The Sportsman's Paradise, and it's a true moniker, especially when you think about fishing.

Louisiana seafood production is a major industry, with shrimp being the star of our bounty. Close to fifty percent of the shrimp harvested from the Gulf of Mexico each year is done by Louisiana shrimpers. A festival to celebrate the delicious crustacean started in 1936, but in 1967, after the petroleum business became prominent, the two largest industries joined forces for celebration in Morgan City, Louisiana, and have never looked back. Every Labor Day weekend people migrate to Morgan City to enjoy the Louisiana Shrimp and Petroleum Festival where shrimp is king.

Over on the Westbank at the shrimp market, booth after booth of family fishermen offer their fresh catch. Shrimp is divided by size and sold by weight. With the Gulf just a mere 50 miles away as the crow flies, New Orleans has access to some of the freshest and finest wild shrimp you'll ever get your hands on. Boat to stall, caught in the morning, and sold a few hours later.

Growing up, Mom frequently made fried shrimp po' boys on Fridays. And during the week, we'd always have some kind of shrimp and pasta dish with a creamy sauce. I would help Mom peel the fresh shrimp, and as we were peeling, she put the shells in a pot to boil. That's the shrimp stock she froze for later use. She would divide the peeled shrimp to set aside for her meal plans of the week. After boiling the shells, they were so clean they could go right in the trash and you'd never know they were there.

Some people might say "Wow, you were rich with shrimp twice a week!" I'll tell ya a little secret. If that's the measure of richness then all of us down here in New Orleans are millionaires.

KEVIN'S TAKE

The worst thing you can do is overcook a shrimp. Just remember, it takes about a quick second to cook them. If the shrimp curls and turns pink, it's done. No need to second guess it. If you are making a sauce or a gumbo or even a pasta dish, you add the shrimp for the very last couple of minutes of cooking time. It's that easy.

SHRIMP NACHOS

Serves 4

Vegetable oil, for frying

24 (8-inch) tortillas

1/2 cup diced red onion

1/2 cup diced red bell pepper

1 jalapeño, seeded and diced

4 Roma tomatoes, diced

1/2 cup chopped cilantro, divided

2 tablespoons lemon juice

1 teaspoon kosher salt

4 tablespoons butter

1 pound shrimp, peeled
and deveined

2 tablespoons Creole seasoning

1 tablespoon minced garlic

1 teaspoon cumin

2 cups grated Mexican
cheese blend

Sour cream, to taste

Preheat oil to 375 degrees. Cut tortillas in quarters and fry in oil for 1 minute until crisp. Drain on a paper towel-lined plate and sprinkle with salt.

In a bowl, mix onion, bell pepper, jalapeño, tomatoes, 1/4 cup cilantro, lemon juice, and salt. Let salsa set for 30 minutes.

Melt butter in a skillet over medium heat. Add shrimp, Creole seasoning, garlic, and cumin.

Cook for 5 minutes or until shrimp turn pink and are cooked through.

To assemble, place tortilla chips on platter and sprinkle salsa over chips. Spoon shrimp on next and top with cheese. If you wish you can place under broiler for 2 minutes to melt cheese. Garnish with sour cream and remaining cilantro.

SHRIMP AND GRITS

Serves 4 to 6

GRITS

2 cups chicken stock

3 cups milk

1 teaspoon kosher salt

1 cup stone-ground grits

4 tablespoons butter

1 to 2 cups grated sharp white cheddar cheese, preferably smoked

Salt, to taste

SHRIMP

5 thick bacon slices, chopped

1 to 1½ pounds jumbo shrimp, peeled and deveined

1 tablespoon Creole seasoning

1 teaspoon kosher salt

2 tablespoons chopped parsley

2 teaspoons minced garlic

2 green onions, thinly sliced

½ cup diced red bell pepper

1 teaspoon smoked paprika

¼ cup shrimp or chicken stock

1 tablespoon lemon juice

GRITS Add stock, milk, and salt to a heavy saucepan and bring to a boil. Gradually whisk in the grits, a little at a time, stirring continuously to prevent any lumps.

Reduce heat to barely a simmer and cook grits, covered but stirring frequently, until stock is fully absorbed and grits are thickened, about 15 minutes.

Remove grits from heat. Add butter, cheese, and salt, stirring with a whisk until cheese melts.

SHRIMP In a large skillet over medium heat, sauté bacon until brown and crisp, 3–5 minutes.

Remove bacon from skillet and drain on a paper towel-lined plate. There will be some bacon drippings left in the pan. Add shrimp, season with Creole seasoning and salt, then sauté for about 3 minutes. Remove shrimp from pan and set aside.

Add parsley, garlic, green onions, bell pepper, and paprika to the pan; stir in stock. Continue cooking for another 3 minutes. Add shrimp and lemon juice for the last minute of cooking time. Add the bacon and toss.

To assemble the dish, place grits at the bottom of individual shallow bowls and top with shrimp and sauce.

BEER BATTER SHRIMP FRITTERS

Serves 4

---

1 cup warm beer, of choice

1¼ cups all-purpose flour

½ teaspoon cayenne pepper

1 teaspoon kosher salt

½ teaspoon white pepper

2 cups cleaned, deveined, and chopped shrimp

1 tablespoon Creole seasoning

½ cup sliced green onions

¼ cup chopped parsley

½ to 1 teaspoon minced garlic

Vegetable oil, for frying

Lemon wedges, for serving

In a large bowl, mix the beer, flour, cayenne, salt, and pepper together. Set aside for 4 hours.

Put the shrimp in a separate bowl and sprinkle with Creole seasoning. Cover and refrigerate until ready to add to batter.

When you are ready to cook the fritters, mix the shrimp, green onions, parsley, and garlic into the batter.

Heat oil, 2 inches deep, in a heavy skillet over medium-high heat until oil just starts to shimmer, about 375 degrees on a thermometer.

Drop teaspoon-size spoonfuls into the hot oil and cook until golden brown on both sides. Remove from oil and drain on paper towel-lined plate. Serve hot with lemon wedges.

NEW ORLEANS ITALIAN— THE SICILIAN WAY

AS A CHILD, I LOVED SPAGHETTI and meatballs. Trips to Venezia on Carrolton Avenue even today keep me dialed into New Orleans-style Italian cuisine. The red gravy, that's marinara to the rest of the world, is center stage with chicken or eggplant Parmesan. Venezia's traditional menu items are very authentic. They even have an old stone pizza oven. For me, it's lifelong memories of great New Orleans Italian food.

Italian families lived in most neighborhoods around the city. The corner store in my neighborhood was named Maggio's after the Italian family who ran it. It was where we stopped for a quick something we needed at home. But it was the French Quarter that had the most influence from the Italian immigrants.

The Italian influences in New Orleans represent a true melding of culture and cuisine—without losing any authenticity. I've often spoken about the French Quarter being nicknamed "Little Italy" by the locals.

The late nineteenth century brought a tremendous influx of Italian immigrants to the United States, and many came from Sicily. From the steamers docked along the wharfs, Sicilian after Sicilian immigrant stepped into the country for the first time, and brought with them a love of family, food, and culture. See? The Italians share the same sensibilities as New Orleanians. And I think that's why the Italian influence is so prevalent in New Orleans, and can be seen so clearly at the Italian Heritage Festival every April. It is fun to celebrate with the Italian community at the festival, but it is also great to enjoy their influence, and more importantly, taste it all year long at several restaurants in and around the city.

Kevin's Take I think I can safely say that every New Orleanian knows about marinara sauce. We even have a great debate about whether it is called red gravy or red sauce. I may not be sure what each of my friends call it, but what I do know for sure is that we will all happily eat it and use bread to sop any up that may be left on our plate.

We also like marinara's cousin, vodka sauce. This red sauce is made with the addition of cream and vodka. The vodka acts as an emulsifier between the cream and the acidic tomato sauce so they don't separate, and the alcohol almost completely cooks out but leaves a distinct and delicious flavor.

FRIED CALAMARI
WITH CREAMY LEMON BUTTER SAUCE

Serves 2

Vegetable oil, for frying

3 egg whites

1/4 cup cornstarch

1/2 cup all-purpose flour

1 teaspoon Creole seasoning

1 teaspoon kosher salt, plus more

1 teaspoon freshly ground black pepper

1/2 pound calamari rings

Heat oil in a large pot over medium high heat to 375 degrees.

Place egg whites in a bowl, whisk slightly. In another bowl, mix together cornstarch, flour, Creole seasoning, salt, and pepper.

Dip calamari rings into egg then place in dry mixture and toss to coat. Shake any excess off.

Depending on the size of your pot, you may need to fry the calamari in batches. Be careful not to crowd the pan or the calamari will stick together. Fry calamari for 2 minutes. Do not overcook or it will become tough. Using a slotted spoon, transfer to a paper towel-lined plate. Sprinkle with a little more salt, if desired. Serve with Creamy Lemon Butter Sauce.

CREAMY LEMON BUTTER SAUCE *Makes 1 cup*

1/2 cup white wine

1 shallot, minced

1 cup butter, cut into pieces

1/4 cup whipping cream

Juice of 1 lemon

In small saucepan, heat wine and shallot. Bring to a boil and reduce mixture over medium-high heat until only 2 tablespoons of liquid remain.

Reduce heat to low and whisk in butter, a few pieces at a time, until sauce is smooth and all the butter is incorporated. Whisk in cream and lemon juice. Keep warm in the top of a double boiler set over hot water until serving time.

SAUSAGE AND PEPPER CALZONE

Serves 4

1/2 pound hot Italian sausage, casings removed

1/2 cup thinly sliced red bell pepper

1/2 cup thinly sliced green bell pepper

1 cup thinly sliced yellow onion

3 cloves garlic, minced

1 teaspoon Creole seasoning

1 teaspoon kosher salt

1 pound store-bought frozen pizza dough, thawed and room temperature

All-purpose flour, as needed

1/2 cup ricotta cheese

1 1/2 cup grated mozzarella cheese

1 large egg

1 tablespoon water

1/2 teaspoon finely chopped fresh rosemary

Sea salt, to taste

Position a rack in the center of the oven. Put a pizza stone or an upside down baking sheet on the rack and heat the oven to 450 degrees. Line a pizza peel or a flat baking sheet with parchment paper.

In a large nonstick skillet, cook the sausage, peppers, onion, and garlic over medium-high heat, stirring and breaking up the sausage, until the sausage browns and the peppers and onion soften, about 5 minutes. Season with Creole seasoning and salt. Remove from the heat and let cool slightly.

Divide the dough into 4 equal pieces. Lightly flour a work surface. Using your hands or a rolling pin, stretch each piece into a 6- to 7-inch round.

Divide the ricotta among the 4 rounds, placing it on one half and leaving a little room around the edge. Top with the sausage and pepper mixture and the mozzarella. Fold the dough in half over the filling. Pinch and crimp the edges of the dough with a fork or your fingers to tightly seal.

In a small bowl, whisk the egg with water. Brush over the calzones and sprinkle with the rosemary and a little sea salt. Transfer to the parchment-lined peel. Slide the parchment and calzones onto the hot pizza stone and bake until golden on top and bottom, 10–14 minutes, rotating halfway through baking.

MEATBALL PO' BOY
WITH VODKA SAUCE

Serves 10

---

2 pounds lean ground beef

3/4 pound ground Italian sausage

4 large eggs

1 cup grated Parmesan cheese

1/2 cup Italian breadcrumbs

1/4 cup chopped parsley

1/2 tablespoon chopped basil

1 tablespoon Creole seasoning

1 teaspoon kosher salt

1 teaspoon garlic powder

1/4 teaspoon black pepper

2 loaves po' boy or French bread

Vodka Sauce, for
dressing sandwich

10 slices baby Swiss cheese

Preheat oven to 350 degrees.

In a large bowl, mix together the beef, sausage, eggs, Parmesan cheese, breadcrumbs, parsley, basil, Creole seasoning, salt, garlic powder, and pepper.

Roll into 1 1/2-inch balls and place close together in greased 9 x 13-inch pans. Bake

for 35 minutes or until the meatballs are cooked through.

To serve, cut open bread, making sure not to cut all the way through, spoon on meatballs and Vodka Sauce, and top with Swiss cheese. Slice into 10 servings.

VODKA SAUCE *Makes 4 cups*

3 tablespoons olive oil

1 cup chopped sweet onion

4 cloves garlic, minced

1/4 teaspoon red pepper flakes

1 (28-ounce) can whole
peeled tomatoes

1/3 cup vodka

1 tablespoon tomato paste

1 tablespoon balsamic vinegar

1 teaspoon kosher salt

1 teaspoon pepper

1/4 cup chopped basil

3/4 cup half-and-half

2 tablespoons grated
Parmesan cheese

continued

In a large skillet, heat olive oil over medium heat. Add onion and garlic and cook for 3 minutes.

Add red pepper flakes and cook for 1 minute. Stir in tomatoes and vodka and continue cooking for 5 minutes, stirring occasionally. Then add in tomato paste, vinegar, salt, and pepper; stir to combine. Reduce heat to low and simmer, partially covered, for 20 minutes, stirring occasionally.

Transfer tomato mixture to a food processor, add basil, and purée until smooth. Return sauce to pan and stir in half-and-half over low heat. Cook until warmed through, about 2 minutes. Remove from heat and stir in Parmesan cheese.

CAJUN COOKING CULTURE

MY GRANDMOTHER EMILY was from Lafourche Crossing just outside of Thibodaux, Louisiana. Grandpa was born in Berwick, just across the river from Morgan City. Folks, this is the heart of Cajun country. Grandma Emily spoke fluent French. I'm not sure if Grandpa Oscar spoke French or not, because he was really quiet. He was more of a head nodder and an "uh huh" person. But when he spoke, you listened up because it was going to be funny. That's how my dad was. I think I get my sense of humor from them. And I know I get my ability to make a Cajun roux from Grandma Emily.

Just to be clear, my grandparents were not Cajuns. They were Creoles living in Cajun country. But the local cooking style and ingredients really influenced how my grandmother cooked. Once I got into the culinary business and started working daily with New Orleans food and ingredients, I came to have a clearer understanding of the lessons learned in both of my families' kitchens.

Grandma Emily could make a good dark roux. Her roux recipe, and the understanding of how she consistently made a nuanced and perfect roux, are two of the greatest culinary gifts I've ever received. Her roux was really my first introduction to Cajun flavors. And when I began touring Cajun country leading groups on culinary excursions, I never felt out of place. The food and the food styles were always familiar. She was an expert at melding the styles of Cajun and Creole together without losing authenticity.

One of the other lessons the Belton side of the family taught me was the difference between a Bayou Cajun and a Prairie Cajun. Folks in Thibodaux are Bayou Cajuns. Their gumbo and étouffée are made with seafood, and they don't mix seafood with other meats. The Prairie Cajuns, who are more centralized around Lafayette, do gumbos with meat and andouille. You'll find rabbit, duck, and sausage in their jambalaya. It's an interesting fact that adds some layers of intrigue to how Cajun cuisine and styles of cooking ebb and flow between families.

KEVIN'S TAKE

South Louisiana is basically like a foreign country. If you really want to experience a part of U.S. culture unlike any other spot, just cross the Mississippi River and take Highway 90 south. You go through Cajun country and pass through towns like Houma, Thibodaux, Morgan City, New Iberia, St. Martinville, and Breaux Bridge before you end up in Lafayette. You can follow guides like the Cracklin Trail or the Boudin Trail, and whichever trail you map out, plan to stop at as many local-looking gas stations as you can. That's where you'll find an array of Cajun-style quick foods that will knock your socks off. There is a surprise around every corner.

CAJUN FRIED FROG LEGS

Serves 8

---

16 frog legs, skinned and cleaned

3 tablespoons Creole seasoning, divided

3 eggs, beaten

½ cup milk

½ cup all-purpose flour, plus more for dusting

¼ cup yellow cornmeal

1 teaspoon kosher salt

1 teaspoon paprika

1 teaspoon onion powder

1 teaspoon garlic powder

½ teaspoon cayenne pepper

¼ teaspoon black pepper

¼ teaspoon white pepper

1 cup canola or peanut oil

Rinse frog legs well and pat dry. Sprinkle 2 tablespoons Creole seasoning on the legs. In a glass bowl, mix the eggs and milk.

In another bowl, combine flour, cornmeal, remaining Creole seasoning, salt, paprika, onion powder, garlic powder, cayenne, black, and white peppers.

Take the seasoned frog legs and lightly coat with a dusting of flour. This helps the egg mixture stick to the legs. Dip the legs into egg mixture then dredge in the seasoned flour mixture until the legs are fully coated.

Heat oil in a large skillet and fry frog legs until golden brown, 6–8 minutes. Drain on paper towels and serve.

CATFISH COURTBOUILLON

Serves 4 to 6

4 strips bacon, chopped

2 cups chopped onions

2 cups chopped green bell peppers

1 cup diced celery

2 tablespoons minced garlic

1/2 cup chopped parsley

1 teaspoon dried thyme

1 jalapeño, seeded and diced

2 cups diced tomatoes

2 tablespoons Dry Roux Flour ("Dry Roux Flour" on page 111)

4 cups seafood stock

2 bay leaves

1 tablespoon Creole Seasoning

1 teaspoon kosher salt

1/2 teaspoon black pepper

1 teaspoon hot sauce

2 pounds catfish fillets, cut into large pieces

4 cups cooked long-grain white rice

1 cup sliced green onion

In a Dutch oven over medium-high heat, brown bacon, about 5 minutes. Remove the bacon and drain on a paper towel-lined plate.

In the same Dutch oven, add the onions, bell peppers, and celery to the bacon grease and sauté until browned. Reduce the heat and add the garlic, parsley, thyme, jalapeño, and tomatoes. Stir to incorporate and add Dry Roux Flour and the stock. Stir the mixture and add the bay leaf and bacon pieces along with the Creole seasoning, salt, pepper and hot sauce. Cover and let cook at a simmer for 40 minutes, stirring occasionally.

Uncover the pot and taste the mixture; adjust seasoning to your taste. About 15 minutes before serving, submerge the catfish fillets into the sauce and cover. Cook at a simmer until the catfish is tender, about 10 minutes. Turn off the heat and let rest, covered, for 5 minutes before serving.

For plating, mound a large portion of rice in the center of a plate or shallow bowl and spoon the courtbouillon sauce and catfish around the rice. Sprinkle with green onion.

CRACKLINS

Makes 3 to 5 pounds cooked cracklins

Vegetable oil, for frying

8 pounds pork belly, cut into 1-inch squares

Creole seasoning, for sprinkling

Fill a large cast iron pot halfway with oil and heat over medium heat until the oil reaches 375 degrees.

Add the pork belly to the oil and cook, stirring constantly, until golden brown and the skins begin to float, crack, and pop, about 1 hour. Drain on a sheet pan lined with paper towels and allow to cool for 30 minutes.

Heat the oil to 375 degrees again and fry a second time, stirring occasionally, until the cracklins are crisp and golden, 10–12 minutes. Drain on a sheet pan lined with paper towels. Sprinkle liberally with Creole seasoning and serve for snacking.

CELEBRATING LATIN INFLUENCE

NEW ORLEANS HAS A VIBE. It's that vibe that brings people from all over the world to eat and listen to music. We've become famous for our vibe. Our vibe is unlike anyplace else. It's taken 300 years and generations of mixing and mashing of cultures, religions, politics, and more to create New Orleans.

You feel that vibe strongly when you walk the streets of the French Quarter, Treme, Marigny, Bywater and 7th Ward. It's a different vibe than Algiers Point, the Garden District, and Uptown. It's an older, historic kind of vibe. It's a culture vibe. It's French and it's Spanish.

My wife Monica hails from Colombia. In my opinion, Monica is one of the best cooks around. And she works very hard to bring her culture home through traditional cooking methods. Like the Spanish, French, and Creoles before her, she has learned to make due with ingredients that might not be traditional in her family recipes.

We take every opportunity to explore Latin-style restaurants across New Orleans. Be it tapas at a Spanish restaurant Uptown, arepas in a family-run spot on Carondolet Street, or a mole sauce at a traditional Mexican restaurant on Carrolton Avenue in Mid-City, we are out there trying everything. With Monica, a whole new culinary world opened up for me. I became aware of parallels between Latin foods and Creole and Cajun fare. And even though it makes perfect sense, it's nonetheless exciting to learn about the cultural culinary connections.

For example, I've learned that depending on the country or origin, arepas can be thick or thin and are made with refined, precooked corn flour and filled with a variety of different ingredients. The filling used inside arepas depends on geography. Seafood-filled arepas come from coastal towns whereas meat-filled arepas are found inland or in mountainous regions. It's like Creole style versus Cajun style.

Kevin's Take
Like all cultures and unique places, the spirit is fully experienced by ordering and tasting traditional foods. Can you imagine coming to New Orleans and missing out on gumbo or étouffée? I suggest next time you go to a restaurant that strongly represents a culture or a country that you ask your server what item on the menu would be most likely found at grandma's house, and then order it. Works for me every time.

PATATAS BRAVAS
WITH GARLIC AIOLI

Serves 4

POTATOES

½ teaspoon baking soda

1 teaspoon kosher salt

2½ pounds Yukon gold potatoes, cut into a ¾-inch dice

¼ cup olive oil

1 teaspoon kosher salt

1 tablespoon Creole seasoning

GARLIC AIOLI

½ cup good quality mayonnaise

2 cloves garlic, grated or pressed

1 tablespoon lemon juice

Salt and pepper, to taste

POTATOES Place a large cast iron skillet in cold oven and preheat oven to 500 degrees.

Add baking soda and salt to a pot of water and bring to a boil. Add potatoes, cover, and bring back to boil. As soon as the water is boiling, set a timer for 1 minute. When the timer goes off, immediately drain the potatoes in a colander, discarding the water.

Return potatoes to the pot and stir for 30 seconds then add olive oil, salt, and Creole seasoning; stir to make sure potatoes are fully coated.

Carefully remove hot skillet from oven and pour potatoes into the skillet, arranging them in a single layer. Return to oven and bake for 15 minutes.

Remove skillet from oven and use a spatula to flip the potatoes. Return to the oven for another 15–25 minutes, until potatoes are golden and crispy.

GARLIC AIOLI Add mayonnaise, garlic, and lemon juice to a bowl and stir to combine. Add salt and pepper.

TO SERVE Drizzle aioli over potatoes and serve with more sauce on the side for dipping, or serve aioli on the side. Top with fresh chopped parsley for garnish, if desired.

SWEET POTATO EMPANADAS

Serves 4

DOUGH

1 cup butter, room temperature

1 (8-ounce) package cream cheese, room temperature

2½ cups all-purpose flour

¼ teaspoon salt

¼ cup sugar

SWEET POTATO FILLING

1 large sweet potato, peeled and diced

2 tablespoons butter

¼ teaspoon ground cinnamon

4 tablespoons brown sugar

4 tablespoons honey

¼ teaspoon salt

TOPPING

1 egg

1 tablespoon water

½ cup sugar

1 tablespoon ground cinnamon

DOUGH In food processor, add butter, cream cheese, flour, salt, and sugar. Pulse until dough comes together. Turn out dough on a floured surface and gather into a ball. Wrap with plastic wrap and chill for 1 hour. This step can done ahead of time.

SWEET POTATO FILLING In a small pot, add sweet potato and cover with water. Bring to a boil and cook for 20–25 minutes until fork tender. Drain, discarding the water, and add sweet potato back into pot. Stir in butter, cinnamon, brown sugar, honey, and salt. Mash with wooden spoon or potato masher. Place mixture in the refrigerator to cool for about 1 hour.

Preheat oven to 375 degrees. Line a baking sheet with parchment paper.

Lightly flour your work surface and roll out dough to ¼ inch thick. Using a 3-inch round cutter, cut out the dough into as many rounds as you can get. Place 1 teaspoon of filling in middle of each round, fold over, and press edges together then crimp with a fork.

Whisk whole egg and water together for the egg wash. Place empanadas on the prepared baking sheets and brush with egg wash. Mix sugar and cinnamon together and sprinkle on empanadas. Bake for 25 minutes. Remove from oven and let cool for 10 minutes before serving.

CEMITA POBLANA
(PUEBLA-STYLE SANDWICH)

Serves 4

---

1 cup all-purpose flour

4 eggs, beaten

1 cup breadcrumbs

4 (¼-inch-thick) veal cutlets

2 tablespoons Creole seasoning

1 teaspoon kosher salt

¼ cup vegetable oil

4 round rolls, split and toasted

2 avocados, pitted, peeled, and thinly sliced

12 ounces queso blanco or mozzarella cheese, grated

8 thin slices yellow onion

8 canned chipotle chiles in adobo, finely chopped, plus 3 tablespoons sauce

Place flour, eggs, and breadcrumbs each in a separate shallow dish. Season veal with Creole seasoning and salt then coat with flour, shaking off excess. Dip veal in eggs then dredge in breadcrumbs. Set aside.

Heat oil in a large skillet over medium-high heat, and cook veal cutlets, turning once, until golden brown on both sides, about 6 minutes. Transfer to paper towels to drain.

Place 1 veal cutlet on the bottom half of each roll and top with half an avocado, ¼ of the cheese, 2 slices onion, and ¼ of the chipotle chiles with sauce. Cover with top bun and serve.

THE NEW ORLEANS BURGER

MY DAD WAS THE FIRST PERSON I ever saw take a crab cake and turn it into a burger. He would pack the leftover crab cakes, dressing them just like Mom's Saturday burgers, for his lunch. It gives me great delight to see something like Dad's crab burger on an upscale restaurant menu. My parents loved food, and the creativity they put in our meals just astounds me even today.

I always anticipated if Mom was not in the kitchen working on supper, that meant Dad and I would go on a burger run. He and I would go to the corner of Prytania and Louisiana to the Royal Castle. We were sent for a dozen of the petite, thin patty "castle" burgers. Royal Castle packed them like a box of donuts. What nobody knew, especially Mom, was that Dad almost always ordered eighteen burgers—six for us to eat on the way home. Our little secret.

Mom also had a secret—how to make an incredible burger. She would buy different cuts of meat and have the butcher grind them together for her burgers. I remember him asking her if she wanted it ground once or twice. Burger meat was ground once, for less mixing and keeping the fat intact, and meatloaf and filling meat was ground twice, breaking down the less-expensive cuts and combining the fat for more flavor and moisture.

Mom made patties that were loosely packed. She wanted to keep the fats evenly distributed and she knew that over packing the meat would make the burgers turn out dry. Her signature burger was a thin patty seasoned with super finely diced onion and salt and pepper. She cooked them in a hot cast iron skillet.

When Mom "dressed" the burgers, she did it from the top down. The bottom bun was always plain, no vegetables, no condiments. Then the meat topped with cheese went on the bun, followed by crisp chilled vegetables. The bottom bun soaked up the meat juices, leaving you with a soft bun, hot meat, melty cheese, and cool vegetables. Still to this day, I judge burgers on Sarah Belton's culinary standard.

Kevin's Take

Ask the butcher at your grocery store to grind your meat fresh for you to make burgers. And keep the fat. If you trim the fat away, you lose a flavor element.

BACON MONSTER BURGER

Serves 8

---

2 pounds lean ground beef

1 pound bacon, chopped
   and cooked until crisp

2 tablespoons Creole seasoning

2 teaspoons kosher salt

1 teaspoon black pepper

2 teaspoons garlic powder

1 tablespoon vegetable oil

8 slices white cheddar cheese

8 slices Oven-Roasted Crispy
   Pork Belly (below)

8 lettuce leaves

8 slices tomato

Pickles

8 buns, toasted

Bacon Jam (page"Bacon Jam
   Make 2 cups" on page 183)

In a large bowl, combine beef, bacon, Creole seasoning, salt, pepper, and garlic powder. Form mixture into 8 equal-size rounds.

Heat a large cast iron skillet over medium heat. When warm, add oil and meat rounds and immediately press flat using a spatula. Cook for about 3 minutes until browned. Flip over, add cheese, and cook for another 3 minutes.

Remove burgers to a plate and add sliced pork belly to pan, cooking for 1 minute per side. Remove and place on plate with burgers.

To assemble, place lettuce, tomato, and pickles on bottom buns. Top with burgers and slices of pork belly. Schmear top buns with bacon jam and place on top of burgers.

OVEN-ROASTED CRISPY PORK BELLY *Serves 8*

1 pound skinless pork belly

2 teaspoons kosher salt

2 teaspoons sugar

1 teaspoon black pepper

Season pork belly with salt, sugar, and pepper. Cover and refrigerate overnight.

Preheat oven to 450 degrees.

Roast pork belly for 30 minutes, fat side up. Reduce heat to 275 degrees and roast for 1 hour or more, until tender but not mushy. Remove

from oven and let cool to room temperature. Wrap tightly in plastic wrap and refrigerate until chilled through—at least 3 hours and up to 2 days.

Once chilled, slice into thick pieces and brown in a small amount of oil for serving.

BACON JAM *Make 2 cups*

1 pound thick-cut bacon

2 sweet onions, quartered and thickly sliced

$^1/_2$ cup brown sugar

$^1/_3$ cup strong-brewed coffee

$^1/_2$ cup water

1 tablespoon balsamic vinegar

Cut the bacon into half-inch slices and add them to a large frying pan. Don't worry if the bacon pieces stick together; they will come apart as they fry. Cook over medium-high heat for about 10 minutes, stirring frequently, until the bacon is cooked but still quite chewy. A few crispy bits are okay.

Using a slotted spoon, remove the bacon from the pan and set aside on a paper towel-lined plate. Pour out all but 1 tablespoon of the drippings and reserve for another use.

Add the onions to the pan and cook for 8–10 minutes then reduce the heat to low. Add the brown sugar and stir. Continue to cook until the onions have caramelized, about 20 minutes. Add the coffee, water, and the reserved bacon and increase the heat to medium. Continue to cook, stirring every 5 minutes, until the onions are thick and jam-like, about 30 minutes.

Remove from heat and stir in the vinegar. Add salt, if necessary. Use immediately or refrigerate for up to 1 week. Bring back to room temperature before serving.

SHRIMP AND CRAB BURGER

Serves 6

½ pound raw shrimp,
  peeled and deveined

½ pound claw crabmeat

¾ cup breadcrumbs

¼ cup finely diced red bell pepper

3 tablespoons chives, sliced,
  plus more for garnish

1 tablespoon Creole seasoning

½ teaspoon kosher salt

¼ teaspoon cayenne pepper

2 eggs

1 teaspoon lemon zest

4 tablespoons olive oil

Sliced tomato

Lettuce

6 buns, toasted

Sour cream

Lemon wedges, garnish for serving

Place the shrimp in food processor. Pulse until coarsely chopped, being careful not to grind into a paste. Transfer the shrimp to a large bowl and add crabmeat, breadcrumbs, bell pepper, 3 tablespoons chives, Creole seasoning, salt, cayenne, eggs, and lemon zest. Stir gently to combine.

Form the mixture into 6 patties.

Heat the olive oil in a large pan over medium-high heat. Add the patties in a single layer and cook for 4–5 minutes on each side or until golden brown.

Serve immediately with sliced tomato and lettuce on toasted buns, topped with a dollop sour cream, if desired. Garnish with lemon wedges.

TRIPLE CHEESY CHEESE BURGER

Serves 8

1 pound ground beef

½ cup grated cheddar cheese

½ cup grated Gruyère cheese

1 tablespoon Creole seasoning

1 teaspoon kosher salt

½ teaspoon cracked black pepper

1 teaspoon garlic powder

2 tablespoons vegetable oil

16 Macaroni Buns

8 thin slices onion

Pickles

In a bowl, mix ground beef and cheeses together. Divide into 8 equal-size balls.

In a small bowl, mix Creole seasoning, salt, pepper, and garlic powder together. Season each ball with seasoning mix.

Heat large cast iron skillet over medium heat and add oil. Place a ball of beef in the pan and press flat with a spatula. Cook until browned, about 3 minutes, and flip, cooking another 3 minutes. To serve, place beef patties between 2 macaroni buns with a slice of onion and pickles.

MACARONI BUNS

4 tablespoons butter

2¼ cup all-purpose flour, divided

3 cups evaporated milk

2 tablespoons Creole seasoning

1 teaspoon kosher salt

¼ teaspoon cayenne pepper

2 tablespoons finely minced garlic

1 pound macaroni, cooked

1 cup cubed sharp cheddar cheese

1 cup cubed white cheddar cheese

1 cup cubed pepper jack cheese

1 cup grated mozzarella cheese

Vegetable oil, for frying

3 eggs, beaten

¼ cup milk

2 cups breadcrumbs

In a large pot, melt the butter over medium heat. Sprinkle in ¼ cup flour and stir until combined. Add the milk and bring to a simmer. Season with Creole seasoning, salt, cayenne, and garlic. Whisk to incorporate and remove any lumps.

Add macaroni to sauce and stir to combine. Fold cheeses into pasta. Pour the mixture into a parchment paper-lined baking dish and freeze for 2 hours.

Cover the bottom of a large skillet with a least ¼ inch of oil. Heat over medium heat. Using a round biscuit cutter about the size of your burgers, cut macaroni and cheese into rounds.

In 3 separate shallow bowls, place 2 cups flour, eggs combined with milk, and breadcrumbs.

Dredge rounds in flour, then egg wash, and finally breadcrumbs, shaking off excess. Fry rounds for about 2 minutes per side until golden brown. Drain on a paper towel-lined plate.

INDEX

METRIC CONVERSION CHART

Volume Measurements		Weight Measurements		Temperature Conversion	
U.S.	**Metric**	**U.S.**	**Metric**	**Fahrenheit**	**Celsius**
1 teaspoon	5 ml	½ ounce	15 g	250	120
1 tablespoon	15 ml	1 ounce	30 g	300	150
¼ cup	60 ml	3 ounces	90 g	325	160
⅓ cup	75 ml	4 ounces	115 g	350	180
½ cup	125 ml	8 ounces	225 g	375	190
⅔ cup	150 ml	12 ounces	350 g	400	200
¾ cup	175 ml	1 pound	450 g	425	220
1 cup	250 ml	2¼ pounds	1 kg	450	230